Praying For A Whole New World

Gospel Sermons For Advent/Christmas/Epiphany Cycle C

William G. Carter

CSS Publishing Company, Inc., Lima, Ohio

PRAYING FOR A WHOLE NEW WORLD

Scriptures quotations are from the *New Revised Standard Version of the Bible,* copyright
1989 by the Division of Christian Education of the National Council of the Churches of
Christ in the USA. Used by permission.

Library of Congress Cataloging-in-Publication Data

Carter, William G., 1960-
    Praying for a whole new world : Gospel sermons for Advent/Christmas/Epiphany,
Cycle C / William G. Carter
        p. cm.
    ISBN 0-7880-1728-4 (alk. paper)
    1. Advent sermons. 2. Christmas sermons. 3. Epiphany season—Sermons. 4. Bible.
N.T. Gospels—Sermons. 5. Presbyterian Church—Sermons. 6. Sermons, American. 7.
Lectionary preaching. I. Title.
BV4254.5.C37   2000
252'.61—dc21

00-035798
CIP

This book is available in the following formats, listed by ISBN:
    0-7880-1728-4   Book
    0-7880-1729-2   Disk
    0-7880-1730-6   Sermon Prep

For more information about CSS Publishing Company resources, visit our website at
www.csspub.com.

PRINTED IN U.S.A.

To David and Julie Carter,
who enjoy the Child for whom we've been waiting

Table Of Contents

Introduction

A history professor told me that the earliest Protestants in America discouraged the celebration of Christmas. "It's too much fun," the Puritans reasoned, "and the Gospel of Jesus Christ requires our utmost seriousness."

These days, anybody who talks like that may be mistaken for Ebenezer Scrooge. Fun and celebration are taken as inalienable rights of American citizenship. It's especially true at a time of the year we blithely call "the holidays." The calendar is full of concerts and Christmas parties. We have lights to put up and cards to address. Every December, people who take the church seriously must also juggle family expectations, school activities, and toy advertisements.

Is there too much fun? I don't know. But it is increasingly clear to me that Christian people have to make choices about having "too much Christmas." The pressure to keep up with our culture is exhausting, especially for parents with young children. The commercialism is insidious; this year there are even more "Jesus is the reason for the season" trinkets for sale, and some serpentine merchant is laughing all the way to the bank.

Not to be too blunt about it, but perhaps the old Puritans were on to something. While the business community hopes for a profitable "Black Friday," the church hopes for something — or rather, for Someone — far greater. As some children take delight in Santa's deliveries and other children are disappointed that their last minute requests weren't honored, the church announces we have received a Gift of surpassing value that can be opened each day of the year. When holiday celebrations fade into the winter gloom, the church points to the Light that casts no shadow. In the thick of a lot of manufactured fun, we proclaim the birth of Jesus Christ, in whom we find the life of the world.

7

This collection of sermons is offered as a companion for those who wish to take the Gospel seriously during the days of Advent, Christmas, and Epiphany. They are edited transcripts of sermons preached at the First Presbyterian Church of Clarks Summit, Pennsylvania, where I serve as pastor. I say it this way, because sermons are intended to be heard, not read. Truth be told, I am a bit embarrassed that you will be reading personal conversations between a pastor and a congregation that he loves.

As you read these sermons, you may also pick up that it is my regular practice to read the Scripture lesson and then immediately dive into the sermon. There's a theological reason behind it: the spoken sermon arises out of an encounter with a written text. Like a jazz musician, the preacher creates new melodies from established material. Some run as counterpoint, others enlarge upon the original tune. For that reason, I encourage you to read each Scripture text before you read each sermon. These sermons did not drop out of the air. Rather I have dug them out of a compost heap of reflection and imagination, all in service to Christ, the Sower of the Gospel.

As my work appears in print, I want to thank my daughters Katie and Meg. Their bright eyes display the anticipation and delight of the Christmas season, and their quick smiles are reflections of the Light of the World. Meg and Katie are my pearls of great joy, and they are very patient whenever I disappear to put my sermons together. Now that this book is finished, I must make good on my promise to dance with them to the music of their favorite bluegrass band. Oh, the compromises a father must make!

Another word of gratitude must be offered to the staff and members of First Presbyterian Church. These saints of God continue to challenge and comfort me. They offer the kind of encouragement and rich feedback that any pastor would find helpful, and I am pleased to serve them into a new century.

Whenever I prepare footnotes, I remember my debt to those who speak the truth and tell stories better than I do. A vast company of scholars and colleagues has helped my work and kept me honest. If you scan the notes at the end of each chapter, you will discover the names of some people who have nurtured my faith, sharpened my vision, and given me something to say.

Finally I must thank my family and a wide circle of friends who are very dear to me. They are too numerous to mention and it's too risky to leave out a name. I trust they know who they are, and I will make it my mission to let them know how highly they are regarded. My life has been deeply enriched by their love and support. The best I could ever do is to return something of what they have given me.

WGC
September 1999

Praying For A
Whole New World

Luke 21:25-36

The door slammed. There was a rush upstairs. The man looked at the clock; it was time for his daughter to be home from school. Fourth grade was not going very well, and from the sound of the slam of the door, it had not improved.

He went up to her room and asked about her day. "It was awful," she said, and then she filled in the details. When she unzipped her backpack at school, her homework was nowhere to be found. Her normally charming teacher snarled at the class. The morning dragged on to lunch, when none of the cafeteria choices looked appetizing. The class went outside to the playground and her best friend decided to play with somebody else. To top it off, a big kid named Kevin had made fun of her on the bus.

"It was a rotten day," she sobbed, and he held her. After about ten minutes, she stopped quivering. He rubbed her back and she blew her nose. One more hug, and then he went downstairs.

About a half hour later, he thought it sounded unnaturally quiet, so he sneaked upstairs to see what was happening. To his surprise, she was down on her knees with her hands clasped and her eyes shut, and she was murmuring something.

"Honey," he said, "is everything all right?"

"I'm okay, Daddy, I'm just praying."

"That's good," he whispered. "What are you praying for?"

"Dad, I've decided I don't like this world, so I'm praying for a new one."

Whether she knew it or not, cute as she was, she was rooting herself in thousands of years of Christian tradition. Ever since

11

Jesus appeared among us, Christians have been praying for a whole new world.

That's what lies behind Scripture texts like the one we heard from the twenty-first chapter of Luke. Jesus is speaking about the destruction of Jerusalem. "The day is coming," he says, "when the temple will be dismantled, stone by stone. The city will be circled by armies and people will be forced to flee to the mountains." All that is familiar and settled will be disrupted, and the powers of the heavens will be shaken. And when that happens, Jesus says, "Stand up and raise your heads, because your redemption is drawing near" (Luke 21:28).

He is speaking, I think, about the final arrival of God's kingdom. The day is coming when this old world will pass away and a new creation will be given to us. Fear, fainting, and foreboding will give way to the power and glory of the Son of Man. Confusion and distress among the people of God will turn to trust and security. Every tear will be dried. Every heart will be mended. And no fourth grader will ever again have a terrible, awful, no-good day.

This is our Advent hope: a new world of wholeness and joy. It will literally be a *whole* new world. Jesus reminds us this new world will come only after the old world has passed away.

We have no problem imagining the end of the world. Every year, the movie industry cranks out disaster films about global destruction. Maybe it is a spy thriller, where a reckless villain seeks world domination with no regard for loss of life. Or we buy tickets to watch a technicolor asteroid smashing into New York City. The threat can come from above, as aliens hover over the White House and blast it to bits. Or the threat can come from below, as city dwellers destroy themselves in fire and violence. There is no lack of images about the end of the world. What we lack is a picture of the new creation.

Not long ago Hollywood gave us a television miniseries on Noah's Ark. As we have come to expect, some scriptwriter mixed up the sequence of biblical events, but the essential story stayed the same. A flood wipes out the entire known world. As the book of Genesis says, "The Lord saw that the wickedness of humankind was great in the earth, and that every inclination of the thoughts of

12

their hearts was only evil continually" (Genesis 6:5). So God decided to wash away human wickedness in the waters of a flood. Only Noah's family and pairs of every animal were spared. When the rain began to fall, it looked like the end of the world.

God gives a blessing as the water recedes. The Lord tells Noah and the animals to "be fruitful and multiply." It is a great "do-over" of creation. There is a new opportunity to make good on the original blessing of God. It's the first chapter of Genesis all over again. It looks like a whole new world.

Remember what happens next? Noah gets drunk. A scandal divides his family. A curse is reintroduced into creation. It wasn't a new world after all, but merely a replanting of the old, familiar field.

As Advent begins, we must ask ourselves if we will settle for that. Do we simply want a continuation of what we have seen and known? Or do we hope for something far greater?

In one of her books, Kathleen Norris writes about the hopes of her rural neighbors in South Dakota. The land is frequently harsh and unfruitful, and the people who live there have coined a phrase to underwrite their dreams for the land.

> *"Next-year-country" is a treasured idiom of the western Dakotas, an accurate description of the landscape that farmers and ranchers dwell in* — next year rains will come at the right time; next year I won't get hailed out; next year winter won't set in before I have my hay hauled in for some winter feeding. *I don't know a single person on the land who uses the idea of "next year" as an excuse not to keep on reading the earth, not to look for the signs that mean you've got to get out and do the field work when the time is right.*[1]

Jesus said, "Keep watch over the fig tree and all the trees. Suddenly they sprout leaves and you know the summer is around the bend. In the same way, watch for signs that the kingdom of God is at hand."

It is possible to read some of these signs. Whether it's our own disappointment over a no-good, rotten day, or our disturbance over events on the 11:00 news, we look for God to come and make everything right. Whether we hope for a good corn crop or pray for the power to climb out of a rut, our desire for a new future is God's opportunity to make something new. To make us new. And that is the heart of our Advent hope.

We have to cope with change all the time. There's a man who felt a mid-life crisis coming on. On the precipice of his fiftieth birthday, he announced to his wife, "I feel the need to make a serious change in my life. I can't decide if I want a sports car or an affair."

His wise wife is a marriage and family therapist. She thought for a minute and said, "I recommend the sports car. In the long run, it will be cheaper." So he bought the car.

Sometimes we can make changes that help us cope with the turmoil in our lives. We can buy something or do something, and gain enough time and distance to manage whatever we must. Sooner or later, however, we can't outrun our own weaknesses. Like Noah, we get off the boat and discover we've brought our own baggage on the journey.

The good news for Advent is that we don't have to expect a logical continuation of everything we have already seen and known. Something different is on the way. As theologian Walter Brueggemann notes, "What we ready ourselves for in Advent is the sneaking suspicion, the growing awareness, the building restlessness that this weary world is not the one God has in mind. God will work another world ... according to the person and passion of Jesus."[2] The day is coming when the love and justice of Jesus Christ will fill the universe. According to Jesus, it can only happen after the world as we know it is unplugged and dismantled.

Do we want that?

Sometimes it is so easy to say yes. Think how wonderful it would be to see the end of all the stuff in the world that makes us sick: petty jealousy among family members, mean-spirited backbiting among neighbors, poverty and over-consumption, violence and destruction, racism and hatred. Wouldn't it be nice to get a huge garbage can and throw it all away?

That's what I pray for. Then I am reminded of my own complicity in maintaining the status quo and perpetuating the unbalance of power.

I went out to dinner with friends — mixed greens with balsamic vinaigrette, pine nut crusted chicken with sun dried tomatoes, rice pilaf, summer squash, a bottle of white wine, all followed by chocolate cheesecake. The total bill with tip came to $139.13. The evening was delicious in every way. I went home and turned on the television just in time to see pictures of starving children in Africa. The only words on my heart were, "Lamb of God, have mercy on me."

I took my children to a water park on a hot summer day. All afternoon we slipped and slid down water slides. We splashed in inner tubes and shot down the rapids of a whitewater raft ride. It was the highlight of a great vacation. Still glowing from the experience, I picked up the newspaper to read how a lingering drought back home caused my neighbor's farm to fail. The only prayer I could utter was, "Do over!"

They are small scenes, to be sure, and easily justified to our friends and children. Yet they are signs that can shake the heavens and prepare us for what God has in store. In personal moments like these, the Holy Spirit is God's subversive Advocate. We can expect the Spirit to disrupt us until we are ready to receive what God has prepared for his beloved children and a cherished creation.

As Walter Brueggemann goes on to say:

> *Advent asks if we are bold and sharp enough to speak the hurt that belongs to our weary world. It asks if we are ready and open enough for a newness to be given. It asks if we know the name of the Father to whom we belong, of the Lord whom we confess, of the coming one for whom we wait, and if we trust that one enough to relinquish the old world.*[3]

A whole new world is at hand. All the promises of Scripture will come true. The poor will be filled with good things and the selfish brought down from their thrones. The nations shall beat their swords into plowshares and their spears into pruning hooks. No more shall there be an infant that lives but a few days, or an old person who does not live out a lifetime. The wolf shall lie down with the lamb, the ox and the fatling together. The pure in heart shall see God and the brokenhearted shall dance. God himself will be with us, to wipe every tear from every eye. Death will be no more; mourning and crying and pain will be no more. A piece of bread and a sip of wine will be transformed into a banquet where every hungry guest shall be satisfied.

These are previews of what God promises. They give us glimpses of the whole new world that God intends. The new creation will not come cheaply. Every vested interest in the old order will be challenged by the word of Christ. God will stop at nothing until "the kingdom of this world has become the kingdom of our Lord and of his Christ" (Revelation 11:15).

Even so, come, Lord Jesus!

---

1. Kathleen Norris, *Amazing Grace: A Vocabulary of Faith* (New York: Riverhead Books, 1998), p. 319.

2. Walter Brueggemann, *Proclamation 3: Advent/Christmas (Series B)* (Philadelphia: Fortress Press, 1984), p. 14.

3. *Ibid.*, p. 15.

When The Word Comes To The Wilderness

Luke 3:1-6

You can tell Christmas is on the way when the catalogs start arriving in the mail. Long before the first snowflake falls, there is an avalanche of slick paper flyers. They come as gifts from merchants with toll-free phone numbers, all in the hope that we will buy what they have to offer.

Last year the first catalog came from a company that specializes in Christian home decorations. Like other catalogs, there were smiling snowman doormats and weatherproof gift-wrap for covering the mailbox. On page three, the religious emphasis was revealed in a variety of porcelain créche scenes. Following that, there was an eight-page section of angels, some of which looked a bit pudgy. The catalog showed advent wreathes and hundred-watt stars. And to nobody's surprise, there was absolutely no John the Baptist merchandise.

John is an intruder in our holiday preparations. He splashes cold water on our festivities. Caterers do not serve his favorite menu at our office parties. At a time of year when people dress in their finest clothes, John the Baptist puts on a coat of ragged animal skins. When he speaks, he always interrupts, and then we have to ask him to turn down the volume. If it weren't for the lectionary readings for Advent, we probably wouldn't allow John the Baptist into our sanctuary.

Nevertheless John cries out, "Prepare the way of the Lord! Make his paths straight!" He reminds us of the ancient Advent promise that all flesh shall see the salvation of God. With the clear voice of a prophet, John tells us how to prepare for the coming of

17

God. Straighten the path! Remove the rough spots! Lower the mountains! Lift up the valleys!

It's not that we mind the message — just the messenger. Given the choice, we might want someone else, thank you very much. The most curious thing about the text for today is that Luke insists this message did not come through somebody else.

"In the fifteenth year of the reign of Emperor Tiberius, when Pontius Pilate was governor of Judea, when Herod was ruler of Galilee, and his brother Philip ruler of the region of Ituraea and Trachonitis, and when Lysanias ruler of Abilene ... *the word of God came to John.*"

What a strange contrast! Luke lists five of the most influential leaders of the known world. He gives us a "Who's Who" of first century politics. When God sent the Word to prepare for the coming of Christ, the Word did not go to the halls of power and influence. The Word went to John.

We might want somebody else. Just think: If God had spoken to Tiberius Caesar, the world would have been shaken awake. If God would choose to speak to the powers and the principalities, to the leaders of nations who mobilize armies and pass the laws, if God would only speak to Herod and Philip and Pontius Pilate, we could have a new political order.

Before a national election a few years ago, somebody handed me a "Christian Voter's Scorecard." As he explained, "This scorecard sizes up political candidates on the issues that really matter, like abortion, the freedom to bear arms, and school prayer." The brochure announced that the best candidates said "no" to abortion, "yes" to bearing arms, and "yes" to re-establishing official school prayer. The writers of the scorecard assumed if we could elect the right Christians to office, we could change the government upside-down.

That scorecard saddened me for a number of reasons, not least of which was the assumption that every Christian will vote the same way on those issues. What was even *more* troubling is remembering the strategy has been tried before and it hasn't worked. We elected Jimmy Carter, a Sunday school teacher and a faithful Southern Baptist. In my opinion, President Carter didn't become an effective statesman until he was voted out of office. Only then he was able to accomplish anything of lasting humanitarian value.

"In the fifteenth year of Tiberius Caesar," the Word of God didn't go to Tiberius Caesar. Perhaps an emperor is too involved in running the empire, defending borders, increasing taxes, or voting himself a raise. Those who believe they are in charge of the world are usually too busy to hear the Lord.

No doubt about it, we are experiencing an absence of God in our public life. We speak the Name, but do little to prepare for the Presence. Theological words have been traded for simple slogans, and candidates attend prayer breakfasts only when they want to secure votes. Generally speaking, church attendance continues to decline, and there is nothing any political official can do to reverse the trend. Once you get behind all the technological glitz, you realize there is a deep spiritual void in our land which cannot be filled politically.

Luke says, "The Word of God did not go to the world's politicians ... it went to John."

What Luke goes on to say is even more of a shocker: *"During the high priesthood of Annas and Caiaphas,"* the word of God didn't go to the priests. It went to John. That comes as something of a shock, because people like Annas and Caiaphas handle holy things, think holy thoughts, and perform holy services. Yet God didn't speak to them.

It is a remarkable claim. Annas was the most influential priest of his generation. He cast such a prominent shadow over the Temple that five of his sons attained the office of high priest. So did his son-in-law, Joseph Caiaphas. Together Annas and Caiaphas led the religious life for the entire country of Israel. Wouldn't we expect the Lord to speak to people like them? After all, they serve in the Temple. They light the candles and fiddle with the paraments. They devote their lives to keeping God's commandments and translating them into proper religious deeds.

Yet the Word did not go to them. The very message of God's impending arrival was not entrusted to the priests in the Temple.

How can we explain it? I don't know. It frightens me, for the obvious reason that I have a job like Annas and Caiaphas. Like the priests in the Bible, the people of God expect me to have some measure of ease in handling holy things. It is my job to break the bread in plain view and pour the cup without spilling it. I offer professional guidance to the acolytes, and tell them to light the first two purple candles on the Advent wreath. When nobody else is around, I walk around these holy spaces and never worry about being struck by lightning.

I can't speak for Annas and Caiaphas but I can tell you how it can be behind the stained-glass facade. Did you know it is possible for a minister of God to go through the motions? To act religiously? To merely find the right book, thumb through the pages, and read the right prayer? It is not difficult. In fact, it's fairly easy.

As Eugene Peterson claims in one of his books:

> *For a long time I have been convinced that I could take a person with a high school education, give him or her a six-month trade school training, and provide a pastor who would be satisfactory to any discriminating American congregation. The curriculum would consist of four courses.* Course 1: *Creative Plagiarism. I would put you in touch with a wide range of excellent and inspirational talks, show you how to alter them just enough to obscure their origins, and get you a reputation for wit and wisdom.* Course 2: *Voice Control for Prayer and Counseling. We would develop your own distinct style of Holy Joe intonation, acquiring the skill in resonance and modulation that conveys an unmistakable aura of sanctity.* Course 3: *Efficient Office Management. There is nothing that parishioners admire more in their pastors than the capacity to run a tight ship administratively ...* Course 4: *Image Projection. Here we would master the half-dozen well-known and easily implemented devices that create the impression that we are terrifically busy and widely sought after for counsel by influential people in the community.*[1]

As one preacher speaking to others, Peterson is poking fun, of course, but he is also speaking a hard truth. The clergy always run

20

the risk of merely putting on a good show. Ministers like me can grow so accustomed to the absence of God that we lose our vocabulary for naming God's presence. And we fill the vacuum by heaping up empty prayers and tuning up the religious machinery. The one thing we need is a Word from God. The one gift we cannot purchase out of a catalog is the Word that names us, claims us, judges us, and redeems us. We do not live by bread alone, but by every word that proceeds from the mouth of God.

In the fifteenth year of Tiberius Caesar, God didn't speak to the politicians. During the high priesthood of Annas and Caiaphas, God didn't speak to the religious functionaries. No, *"the word of God came to John, son of Zechariah, in the wilderness."*

And people knew it. When John the Baptist spoke, it was as if God was speaking. They could sense the power. Farmers left their plows in the fields. Merchants left their stores unattended. Everybody came to hear the strange prophet cry out that God was at hand. When they heard John, they knew in their bones that it was true.

Walt Wangerin tells about a woman named Miz Lillian. He never knew what to expect when she shook his hand after worship. On many Sundays she said, "Well, you taught us today." On other Sundays she looked him in the eye. "Hooo, Pastor," she said, "you preached today."

One Sunday, when she reached to shake his hand, Walt held on. "Miz Lillian," he said, "sometimes you say I teach."

"U-huh."

"And sometimes you say I preach."

"Mmm-hmm."

Walt said, "Is there a difference?"

Miz Lillian raised one eyebrow, as if to say, "Didn't they teach you this in seminary?" She said, "Yes, there is."

"What's the difference?"

She said, "When you teach, I learn something for the day. I can take it home and, God willing, I can do it. But when you *preach*, God is here. And sometimes he's smiling, and sometimes he's frowning."[2]

The Word of God came to John. When he preached, everybody knew God was at hand. Sometimes God was smiling and sometimes God was frowning. John's preaching had a profound effect on everybody who heard his voice. "God is at hand," John shouted, and the people knew they could not keep living casual, carefree lives. When you believe God is coming to set things right, you remove the roadblocks to your heart before God blasts them away. When you discover God has something to say, you cannot pretend you are the final authority on anything. *For God is coming!* The valley of shadows will be lifted up. The mountains of pride will be bulldozed to the ground. God will untangle the crooked ways of the heart and polish the rough edges of every available life.

The Word of God came to John. It did not go to the palaces of power where politicians act as if they are in charge of the world. It did not fill the temples of institutional religion, where bored clergy play it safe and nervous worshipers spray extinguishers on holy fire. The Word of God went to the wilderness where winds howl, souls are parched, and hurts are yet unhealed. God spoke where God was needed ... and it made all the difference in the world.

We can hear this Word if our hearts are hungry. We can hear God's promises to give us life and heal our wounds. We can take the bread and drink the cup, and remember how God has made the ultimate sacrifice to claim us for himself.

"All flesh shall see the salvation of God." That's the ancient promise during these days in Advent. It is a Word we can count on. We shall see the salvation of God ... as long as we pass by John the Baptist.

---

1. Eugene Peterson, *Working the Angles: The Shape of Pastoral Integrity* (Grand Rapids: William B. Eerdmans Publishing Co., 1987), pp. 4-5.

2. Walter Wangerin, Jr., *Miz Lil and the Chronicles of Grace* (New York: Harper and Row, Publishers, Inc., 1988), pp. 35-37.

Same Question, Same Answer

Luke 3:7-18

"Preacher, why don't you tell me what you want me to do?" She stood with a frown on her face, while the rest of the church-goers shuffled out the door. The preacher was taken aback. The sermon had seemed to go well. For once, he hadn't tripped over his tongue or turned down an obscure alley. Yet the woman wouldn't let him off the hook.

"I've wanted to ask that question for some time," she said. "As you know, I come to church just about every week. I have heard a lot of interesting sermons, and learned some things about the Bible that I never knew before I began coming to this church. But today, I finally found the words to ask you a question that has nagged at the back of my mind."

"What's that?" said the minister.

She said, "Preacher, why don't you tell me what you want me to do?"

Is there anybody here who has asked the same question? I think so. It is possible to attend worship every week, to sit in these pews and take part in everything that happens, and still go out the door wondering, "So what?"

Or more to the point, it is possible for people like you to come in here, and listen to a minister like me stand up and talk for twenty minutes or so, and when the sermon is over, you say, "What was that all about?" To put it in the words of that woman, "Why don't you tell me what you want me to do?"

It is a sobering challenge for preachers, and it's a good question for the rest of you to ask.

Perhaps you have gone to a meeting where some important topic is discussed and debated. Various points of view are given. A consensus begins to form. Soon, everybody is nodding his or her head in agreement. "Yes, something needs to be done!"

Just then, somebody raises a hand and says, "I move we adjourn." And nothing more ever happens.

Or say, for instance, that you sign up for a class. You've been waiting for that particular topic to be offered. You rearrange your schedule and screen out all other distractions. You give your time to learn about, and analyze, and discuss some very important issue. Before you know it, the class is over, and that's all that ever comes of it. If you're still interested, it is only as an armchair activist.

Or say, for example, you are sitting in church on a Sunday morning. The minister is up front, stomping around in theological muck of his own making. Your mind begins to wander. You start thinking about the roast beef back in the oven, or the fight you had with your teenage daughter about her boyfriend, or whatever it is that you are probably thinking about now. Why does it happen? One reason is because the sermon is not clear. As one of my teachers declared: "A mist in the pulpit becomes a fog in the pew."

Sooner or later, we want the truth pinned down: "Preacher, why don't you tell me what you want me to do?"

That's a good question, especially in the church. In here, we are under the obligation of the gospel to talk about life and death, sin and forgiveness, grace and judgment. Sometimes, particularly after we hear a sermon, we want somebody to put a period on the end of the sentence. Tell us straight out: what does this mean for us?

Now John the Baptist was a preacher. There was fire in his voice as he spoke about life and death, sin and forgiveness, grace and judgment. When people heard John preach they knew that God was swinging the ax at the root of their trees. When John said, "You people are a bunch of snakes," they stood there and took it, because in the depths of their hearts they knew it was true. Yet to their credit, the people who heard John preach were not satisfied with high temperature rhetoric or soft heavenly platitudes. As they heard John speak, the one question that formed on their lips over and over again was this: "What should we do?"

24

The essence of his message is clear, and we regularly hear it at this time of year. John the Baptist points his bony finger at Jesus and says, "This is the One for whom we've been waiting. He is coming to comfort those who are disturbed, and to disturb those who are comfortable. Blessed is he who comes in the name of the Lord. Look at him!"

Then John turns toward you and me and points his finger once again. "Prepare the way," he says. "Straighten out the crooked paths. Flatten the arrogant mountains. Smooth out the splinters in your heart ... or else!"

With that, we look at one another, and then we head to the mall to go shopping.

Let's face it: that's how we prepare for Christmas. We buy a lot of things and we spend a lot of money. When John says, "Prepare the way of the Lord," our first response is to haul out the holly. If there are any crooked paths at this time of year, we throw down a little salt to melt the ice and then we get on our way. We don't have the energy to bulldoze any mountains; most of us are too busy circling the parking lot to find empty spaces. As a merchant once said to me, "You preachers talk about the four weeks of Advent as a time of getting ready for Jesus; but you have to understand — for me, it's a season to move the merchandise."

It's all the more urgent, then, to ask John, "What should we do?" If his sermon essentially points to Jesus as the Coming Messiah, and if he also points to you and me and urges us to prepare for Christ's arrival, then our question is the same as the question of those who first heard John preach. "What should we do?"

John's answer is as bracing for us as it was for his first audience, because the answer has to do with the ways we use or abuse our money. That's right: money! Three times a group of people responds to John's sermon about getting ready for the Messiah. Three times they ask, "What should we do?" Each time John says something specific about money and the power it holds over us.

When John began to preach, a crowd of people came forward and got baptized. They stood up in the Jordan River, their brows still glistening wet, and John gave them his charge. "Give away your extra coats, so that everybody who needs one can have one. Share your food with those who have nothing to eat."

Now, if you know the writings of Luke, you know this is the very picture of God's kingdom. In Luke's second volume, the book of Acts, a man named Peter stands up and preaches a sermon on Pentecost. It cuts people to the heart. They want to know, "What can we do?" (Acts 2:37). Within the next seven verses of that story, all the people were cashing in their extra belongings and sharing the financial proceeds with the poor "as any had need." Luke says they were so filled with the Holy Spirit that there was no room left in their souls for selfishness. They were so generous with one another that "there was not a needy person among them" (Acts 4:34). The name of that group of people was the church.

If somebody is serious about standing in the promised kingdom of Christ, the best evidence is found in that person's ability to share what he or she has. God has no room in the kingdom for a Scrooge or a skinflint, because God himself is not a cheapskate. God gives us Jesus; the very least we can do is share our sweaters and our casseroles with one another.

Draw your own Christmas conclusions from this. When the public school invites us to send in canned food with our children, it's a good idea to do it. We share our food, not merely because it is a nice thing to do, or because we have a few extra dented cans of creamed asparagus in the pantry. No, we share because generosity is an essential mark of the kingdom of God. If the kingdom of God is coming to us in Jesus Christ, then we must respond in generous ways that make it possible for us to belong to the kingdom when it comes — like giving the extra coat or sharing the extra plate of food.

And then, we hear some tax collectors came to get baptized. Perhaps that strikes you as strange, but it does remind us that nobody stands outside the grasp of God. These people are tax collectors. Just picture them coming to the Jordan River to get baptized! I imagine them getting ready to go underwater, holding their noses with one hand and holding up their wallets really high with the other hand. All the time they're saying to themselves, "Yes, Lord, you can have my life, but you're not going to get my pocketbook."

In the first century, a tax collector made his money on the mark-up that he charged his neighbors. According to the system, the right to collect taxes was sold to the highest bidder. One of your neighbors, a Jew, could buy the privilege to take your tax money and give it to the Romans. The collector had to pay all the expected revenue for your town in advance. After that he was free to try to recoup the amount by assessing and collecting whatever tolls he could.[1] If a tax collector could get away with assessing you something extra to feather his own pockets, then that's what he did. You had no recourse but to pay.

So when these tax collectors come up for air and ask, "What should we do?" John speaks so that their whole livelihood is drenched with the holiness of God. If the kingdom of God is at hand, no one can say, "I belong to God," on a Sunday, and then act on Monday morning as if faith is a weekend hobby. So John the Baptist says, "Don't let your greed separate you from the people around you. Take only a fair day's wage, and no more."

Finally, Roman soldiers stepped up and said, "Preacher, what should we do?"

John looked at them, shook his head, and said, "No more of these power games."

They clanked their swords, cleared their throats, and said, "What do you mean?"

John said, "No more manipulation to get your own way. No more threats for the weak. No more extortion, especially for money."

There is no room in God's coming kingdom for those who wish to throw around their power, and take advantage of people who are already feeling worn down. The verb in our text is the word for shaking a fig tree and watching the figs falls to the ground.[2] To put it another way, John says, "No more shakedowns."

This is good advice for any foot soldier who wishes to enlist in the army of the Lord. You cannot act as if you are in charge of the world; the job is already taken. You cannot pretend that everybody needs to bow down before you; somebody else is already seated on the throne. In fact, you can't even demand to get your own way, because God is the One who rules with justice and fierce mercy.

The only people who are fit for the kingdom are the people who are satisfied with God as our ruler.

So having heard all of this, what should we do? I think you know. If we are going to get ready for Christ to come and rule in our hearts, it will involve three things:

- Share your food and clothing with the needy.
- Sidestep every temptation of greed.
- Give up every form of abuse.

This is what God wants from us today. For John the Baptist, as for Jesus who came after him, the words of a sermon must always be translated into deeds of mercy. When the word of the gospel frees us to give generously, to act responsibly, to love willingly, then, indeed, it comes as blessed good news ... and in that moment, we know that the kingdom of God is at hand.

---

1. Joseph A. Fitzmyer, *The Gospel According to Luke I-IX* (New York: Doubleday, 1989), p. 470.

2. Fitzmyer, p. 471.

Two Blessings For An Unwed Mother

Luke 1:39-45 (46-55)

By Christmas vacation of my first year in college, I had become an expert on the birds and the bees. Biology was my major, and after a semester in the freshman class, I was certain that I knew more biology than most adults did in my hometown ... including my minister.

A few days before Christmas, I stopped in to see him. He received me warmly and asked how I had fared in my first semester. "Okay," I replied, skillfully avoiding the subject of my mediocre grades. "But I've come home with some questions."

"Really?" he replied. "Like what?"

"Like the virgin birth," I said. "I've taken a lot of biology, as you know," skillfully avoiding that "a lot" constituted a single course where I received a B-. "And I think this whole business of a virgin birth doesn't make much sense to me. It doesn't fit with what I have learned in biology class."

"What's the problem?" he asked.

"There had to be a father," I announced. "Either it was Joseph or somebody else."

My pastor looked at me with a coy smile and said, "How can you be so sure?"

"Oh, come on," I replied, with all of my newfound expertise. "That's not the way it works. There had to be a father."

My pastor didn't back down. Instead he said something I'll never forget: "So — why not God?"

Why not, indeed? The more we learn, the harder it is to swallow a lot of things that once seemed so palatable. Advent is a season of

29

wonder and mystery. We tell our children stories at this time of year that we would never dare tell when it is warmer and there is more sunlight. The really wise child is the kid who knows how to shut his mouth even when he has a few doubts. But sometimes it is hard to do, especially when you have a whole four months of college behind you.

Doubts can linger with us. These days I find it questionable, for instance, that the child in Elizabeth's tummy "leaped with joy" when the mother of Jesus walked in the room. Elizabeth was six months along in her pregnancy. Pediatricians say that's when Junior starts kicking like a soccer player. No need to make a theological claim about that kick; it seems like it was only a kick.

What's more, I have learned that when two pregnant women find one another, they usually do not talk theology. The conversation turns instead to swollen ankles, stretch marks, morning sickness, or those other unmentionable details which pregnant women discuss when men aren't listening. Ask any pregnant woman and she will probably tell you that a man wrote this story of Elizabeth and Mary. And she would be right.

But when Luke tells this story, he wants to make it clear that God is at work. These are not two typical pregnancies. One woman is as ancient as the Old Testament; the other is a young girl. One is married to a sterile priest, the other — well, she's not actually married yet. The old married woman has a husband who did not believe something like this could actually happen, even though he is a professional guardian of the story of Abraham and Sarah. The young girl, on the other hand, would never make it to college biology class. So she says to the messenger, "Let it happen, just like you say." Her words make all the difference in the world.

We have heard the story of Mary many times. As I hear it this time, it strikes me that perhaps the first person who had a hard time believing the virgin birth was the virgin herself. Biblically speaking, Mary was minding her own business when the angel Gabriel appeared. I don't believe for a minute that she took the news without swallowing really hard.

Consider her circumstances. Historians tell us the average age of a first-time mother in first century Palestine was about thirteen years old. That means Mary was a teenage mother. Few teenagers are ready to become mothers. Most of them are still children themselves.

According to the marital customs of the time, Mary was betrothed to a man named Joseph. The relationship was not a simple engagement that could be made with a ring and a kiss; neither could it be easily broken. By all intents and purposes, Mary already "belonged" to Joseph, even if they weren't quite married. If she told him she was pregnant, it would look like she was admitting to adultery. With an admission like that, he was legally entitled to walk away from her.

From her own lips, she was a "handmaid," a term signifying a peasant of the working lower class. There was no obvious feature to dignify her, no special privilege to set her apart. Luke doesn't say if she was cute with dimples or if she had a 200 I.Q. There is no reason to think that, to the people around her, she was anything more than a poor teenager. In every respect she was an ordinary young woman, until an angel appeared to say, "Congratulations, Mary! You are going to be the mother of the Messiah."

In the story from the first chapter of Luke, her relative Elizabeth responds to that announcement by blessing Mary two different times. The first time Elizabeth exclaimed, "Blessed are you among women!" To this day, Protestants are still trying to figure out the implications of those words. Ever since Elizabeth uttered them, a lot of Christian people have honored Mary. By the third century, theologians were referring to her as "theotokos," that is, "the Mother of God." The woman who gave birth to the Holy Child was, in their thinking, the one who brought God into the world. That's a staggering claim!

But the story seems to give more weight to the second beatitude that Elizabeth uttered. For Elizabeth said, "Blessed is she who believed that there would be a fulfillment of what was spoken to her by the Lord."

"Blessed is she who believed." All the more remarkable, given all the fact that faith doesn't come easy. Most of the time we look for evidence. Where is the evidence that God is alive? The prophet Isaiah says, "I saw an old dead stump the other day, and a shoot was growing out of it." That's all that he saw. The prophet Micah says, "In the dusty little town of Bethlehem, a shepherd will be born." That's it — a new shepherd? Centuries passed without much evidence. As one of my teachers once said, sometimes faith has to survive on one calorie per day.

"Blessed is she who believed." Of course, it's God who makes her faith possible. God sent a baby to Mary. She did not ask for it, did not expect it, or did not know what to do with it. And the baby came anyway. There were days — you know there had to be days — when she wondered why she ever said, "Yes," to an angel. There must have been days when she doubted her own ability as a mother. And there were painful moments when "a sword would pierce her soul." Yet she hung on, because she believed.

That is helpful for me. When I have my doubts, I hang on too, if only because Mary once believed on my behalf. Even when we smugly think we have learned it all, even when we see plenty of evidence to the contrary, Mary is the one who asks us, "So — why not God?"

As someone puts it:

> *We recall Thomas as the exemplar of those who doubt. We see in Peter's denial of Jesus our own weakness and in his reinstatement hope for ourselves. We openly celebrate another Mary (the sister of Martha) for her attentiveness to Jesus' teaching, and we similarly regard the Syrophoenician woman for her persistence. If we can see these people as our predecessors in faith, then perhaps we can also see Mary as the Mother of all Believers.*[1]

Luke underscores the point. Later on in the story, he tells about a woman in a crowd who was taken with the words and deeds of Jesus. When Jesus passed by, she cried out, "Blessed is the womb that bore you and the breasts that nursed you!"

Jesus responds to her, "Blessed rather are those who hear the word of God and obey it!" (Luke 11:27-28).

Jesus was talking, I think, about his mother. Mary heard the word and kept it. She remembered the promises that God made to Israel, and she believed that God remembered them, too. It wasn't enough for her to believe a baby was coming. It wasn't marvelous enough to ponder her pregnancy. No, because of that particular child, she believed in a whole new world. Remember what she sings?

The proud are scattered in the thoughts of their hearts. The powerful brought down from their thrones, the lowly lifted up. The hungry are filled with good things, and the rich are sent away empty. God will remember the promises made to our mothers and fathers.

Her faith was like looking through a telescope. Through the lens she could see things that seem far-off, yet she believed in a God who brings them close at hand. Mary's faith is so confident in the goodness of God that all these merciful deeds sound like a done deal. And in the infinity and eternity of God, they are. *Can you believe it?* That's the question posed each Christmas. *Can you believe that this particular child, born of this particular woman, can turn this particular world upside down?*

Or to put it another way: "So — why not God?"

In a sermon, Martin Luther once said that three miracles happened when Jesus was born in Bethlehem: God became a human being, a virgin conceived, Mary believed. Of these, said Luther, the greatest Christmas miracle was this: Mary believed.[2] Regardless of her low estate as a female in that culture, her virtual anonymity, her human fears and uncertainties, Mary believed. That's why Elizabeth called her "blessed."

Of all the gifts I wish you for Christmas, the one gift I wish more than anything else is the gift of faith. It is the gift of believing that, not only is God able to do wonders out there in the universe somewhere, but that God is able to perform wonders right here — among you and me. It's the hope that was voiced in the prayer of Phillips Brooks:

O holy Child of Bethlehem, descend to us, we pray;
Cast out our sin and enter in, be born in us today.[3]

Blessed is the one who believes it can happen ... right *here*.

1. Beverly Roberts Gaventa, " 'All Generations Will Call Me Blessed': Mary in Biblical and Ecumenical Perspective," *Princeton Seminary Bulletin* 18.3 (November 1997), pp. 260-261.

2. Quoted by William H. Willimon, *Pulpit Resource* 22.4, p. 49.

3. "O Little Town Of Bethlehem," verse 4.

All Is Calm, All Is Bright

Luke 2:1-20

What a time for an angel to forget his lines!
It was the Christmas Pageant at Gravesend, New Hampshire. The Episcopal Church was packed with worshipers, well wishers, and relatives of the cast. Attendance was up, thanks to a positive preview in the local newspaper. The drama critic had reported, "The quintessential Christmas tale, the luster of which has been dulled by its annual repetition, has been given a new sparkle."

One reason for the excitement was the presence of a small boy named Owen Meany. For years his diminutive size had made him a natural for the role of the Announcing Angel. The pastor's wife would hoist him on a rope, where he could swing out of the stage and announce the good news. This year, a much larger boy named Harold Crosby has been assigned the angelic role, and Owen, who was the smallest kid anybody had ever seen, had assumed the role of Baby Jesus.

The moment came when it was time for Harold Angel to descend from the darkness. "Be not afraid!" he said in a quaking voice. Then he repeated it again. "Be not afraid!" When he said those words a third time, it was obvious he had forgotten the rest of his lines. He spun around and faced the back of the stage and said, "Be not afraid" in an indistinct mumble.

Suddenly another voice spoke up. It came from down below, in the hay. The child in the manger knew the forgotten lines, and in a cracked falsetto, his voice rang out. "FOR BEHOLD, I BRING YOU GOOD NEWS OF A GREAT JOY WHICH WILL COME TO ALL THE PEOPLE."

Prompted by the Christ Child, the angel repeated the announcement. And when the spotlight fell on the créche, "the congregation was also prepared to adore him — whatever special Christ this was who not only knew his role but also knew all the other, vital parts of the story."[1]

Tonight is Christmas Eve. All the angels are summoned to tell what they know. Prompted by the birth of Jesus, they announce that something decisive has happened. God has broken through the darkness. A Child has been given to us, to reign in our hearts and to rule the world. The word that best sums up this gift is *peace*.

"Glory to God in the highest heaven, and on earth peace among those whom he favors!"

Maybe we are thinking about peace tonight. A stack of Christmas cards has come to the mailbox. About half of them bear the greeting, "Peace on earth." Peace is a wonderful thing to wish for somebody else. It is a blessed thing for which to hope — primarily because it seems to be in such short supply.

This is December 24, after all. For many people it is the busiest, most erratic day of the year. How many of you were out on the roads this afternoon? Anybody dare to stop at the supermarket? Are your children calm and quiet? This is a night when we could wish for a little peace.

A lot of things might be on your mind tonight. When I was a teenager, I remember one Christmas Eve very distinctly. My family was sitting in our favorite pew. As we lit the candles and sang "Silent Night," my father began to fidget. I turned with a quizzical look and he whispered, "I don't have my shopping done."

As soon as the benediction was over, Dad took us home so Mom could hustle us into bed. Then he blazed a trail for the local Mammon Warehouse to make a few more purchases. The next morning he announced he hadn't been the only one there. Needless to say, my brother, two sisters, and I were glad that he made the trip.

This may be the busiest time of the year. There is so much to do: packages to wrap, places to go, people to see. We might wish for peace.

Even though it is Christmas Eve, for many people in the world it is merely another day. In Africa, eleven million people have died from the AIDS virus, and millions more are at risk. In the horn of Africa, hundreds of thousands have withered to death from famine. In the Balkans, people are still uncovering unspeakable cruelties in their land. There are places in the world where Christmas cease-fires are tentative, and people from both sides of an arbitrary line will carry automatic rifles into worship.

Yet here we are, gathered before red poinsettias and a big green tree. Our choirs have spent weeks tuning up for this one night. The ushers have handed out candles and rounded up a few extra fire extinguishers. We tell familiar stories to our children and sing favorite songs. At the center of all we sing and pray, we dare to claim that "all is calm, all is bright."

We do it, of course, because that is the proclamation of the angels. "Glory to God in the highest heaven, and on earth peace among those whom he favors." At the center of the Christmas story is the announcement that God has given peace to the earth. Peace is not a vain dream or a vague hope. Peace is already here. But what kind of peace are we talking about?

If peace means the ability to get along with others, we are anxious for it. An editorial in a local newspaper asked, "Why can't we stop all the mudslinging in our town?" The writer was referring to borough council meetings, but she could have been describing school board meetings or character assassinations in the church kitchen. Sick of the conflict, she urged a verbal cease-fire for the holidays. "We have to stop fighting and start working together."

If only it could be that easy. If peace were merely a matter of being nice to people with whom we disagree, maybe we could do it. Yet disagreement and discord seem inevitable.

If the peace of Christmas refers to the ability to find some serenity within our own souls, we are ready for it. There are hidden wounds from childhood, which re-emerge this time every year. Life can fracture us. Maybe that's why we have come to church tonight. Perhaps we hope the old stories and favorite songs will bless us with personal peace.

37

Or perhaps we think of peace in global terms. Nations are in pain. Children are hungry. If we could only stop the nations from conspiring and stop the peoples from plotting in vain (Psalm 2:1)!

Yet the peace announced by angels was a different kind of peace. The angels did not announce peace to shepherds who fought with one another. They did not speak to troubled herdsmen whose heads and hearts were divided. And they did not blow their trumpets in the halls of power.

When the angels spoke of peace, they broke the silence from God. They shattered the darkness with news of a savior. From the highest place in the universe, they announced God has come down to make peace with all creation. God has moved toward sinful, destructive people with purely peaceful intentions. Can you understand the depth of that announcement? The angels came to say:

- The God whose name is Mystery has spoken to us;
- The Creator whose actions are more subtle than we can see has kind intentions toward us;
- The One who made heaven and earth has come down among us to redeem and reconcile.

Listen — the angels announced good news for all people. They said, "God has come to you."

What a remarkable thing to say to a group of anonymous shepherds! Shepherds had a hard life. They wandered from place to place and depended on the land for survival. As the shepherds heard the good news, it did not remove them from troubles in the world. When the night is over, they are still nameless. And yet, a word of peace is spoken to them.

It is a remarkable thing for angels to announce to us, because it does not deny the troubles and dangers we face. Neither does it turn aside from the pain still evident in God's creation. God's peace comes in the midst of our trouble and pain to assure us that "all is calm, all is bright." Have you ever experienced that peace?

An elderly woman was going through a great deal of physical pain. Physicians told her that she would not get well. She faced a long painful decline. One night in December, however, a choir of

Presbyterian angels appeared in her driveway to sing carols. She opened the door just in time to hear these words,

> *How silently, how silently, the wondrous gift is given!*
> *So God imparts to human hearts the blessings of his*
>   *heaven.*
> *No ear can hear his coming, but in this world of sin,*
>   *where meek souls will receive him, still*
> *the dear Christ enters in.*[2]

She listened to those words, waved goodbye, and shut the door expecting aches and pains. In that moment, she felt a tranquility she had not known in months. Hobbling up the stairs, the aches and pains returned. Yet something was different.

That is the peace announced to us on Christmas. It is not the absence of pain, but serenity in the midst of stress. Peace is the momentary yet unmistakable awareness that all is right with the world. Peace is the fleeting but very real insight that, beyond all of our troubles, "all is calm, all is bright." As revealed in the skies above Bethlehem, we have a God who loves us, keeps us, and comes to fill us with the peace of the Holy Spirit. The birth of Jesus has changed the world. God has come. If we believe it, if we want to believe it, we are prompted by the Christ Child to join the song of the angels. And we can receive a gift from God that the world cannot give.

Archbishop William Temple once put it this way:

> *Let us at all costs avoid the temptation to make our Christmas worship a withdrawal from the stress and sorrow of life into a realm of unreal beauty. It was into the real world that Christ came, into the city where there was no room for him, and into a country where Herod, the murderer of innocents was king.*
>
> *[Christ] comes to us, not to shield us from the harshness of the world but to give us the courage and strength to bear it; not to snatch us away by some miracle from the conflict of life, but to give us peace — his peace —*

by which we may be calmly steadfast while the conflict rages, and be able to bring to the torn world the healing that is peace.[3]

May the peace of Christ be with you all. Merry Christmas!

---

1. John Irving, *A Prayer for Owen Meany* (New York: Ballantine Books, 1989), pp. 216-217.

2. "O Little Town Of Bethlehem," verse 3.

3. Exact source unknown.

Home For
The Holidays

Luke 2:41-52

Laura was going home for the holidays. As she sat in O'Hare Airport one Christmas morning, she bristled with anticipation. Her vacation would last only two and a half days, but two bags of luggage were stuffed with presents. She had finally gotten the first job that paid any real money, and she was eager to go home and lavish gifts upon people she loved.

Her family met her at the airport and took her back to the familiar neighborhood. The house was bigger than she remembered. They exchanged gifts that evening, and the dutiful daughter kept trying to convince everyone that she hadn't spent too much money. With a lot of laughter and joy, the family moved to the dining room to enjoy a banquet of rich food and wine.

It wasn't long, however, before Laura realized the house to which she returned was no longer the home she knew. The next morning she opened the refrigerator looking for soda water, suddenly remembering her parents would never think to buy it. The cupboard had no bagels or croissants, and the only available jam was full of sugar. Hoping for a caffeine lift, she found only decaffeinated coffee, so she boiled some water for tea.

She was singing along to the radio when her mother walked into the kitchen. "You used to listen to such nice music," her mother said innocently enough. As everyone emerged from their rooms, they gathered in the living room for coffee. Laura told a story, and mentioned an event that happened at a restaurant on the previous Sunday. The conversation stopped for a minute, and she saw judgment in her parents' eyes. A restaurant? On *Sunday?* No comment was made, but the silence spoke volumes. Laura writes:

> *When I again flew home two days later, this time going the other way, I wondered: what did the prodigal son feel like the morning after the party? What would I feel like after this year of freedom, having to move back home? Was that place even home to me any more?*

Then she adds:

> *Home is attractive for many of us precisely because it is irretrievable. If we, like Dorothy, were given a magic pair of ruby slippers to transport us back home at the click of our heels, how many of us would go?*[1]

It's hard to say. On the one hand, Christmas time is family time. The airports bustle with homebound travelers. The college student's beat-up Toyota carries her back to a familiar driveway in a familiar neighborhood. The guestroom in the family homestead is transformed once again into Junior's bedroom, if only for a few days during a holiday vacation. Christmas, like no other time of the year, draws relatives and relations to the same hearth.

Yet Christmas can also expose family relationships to be something less than the Hallmark ideal. When you bring together people who love one another but live together no longer, the reunion can be quite stressful.

It is helpful that Luke tells us a story about the straining of one family's ties. Jesus and his family went to Jerusalem to celebrate a religious festival. Scholars tell us the population of the holy city swelled by thousands during the Passover holiday. Pilgrims traveled from the four ends of the earth. And in the hustle and bustle of such an occasion, Mary and Joseph did not notice that their young son had slipped away.

They assumed he was traveling with friends and neighbors. When Jesus didn't show up at the end of the day, their curiosity turned to fear. Mary and Joseph returned immediately to the city.

They searched frantically for three days before they found him in the Temple, listening to the rabbis.

"Child," said Mary, "why have you treated us like this?" From a parent's perspective, it looked like disobedience. But to hear the young boy Jesus tell it, he was already breaking away from home. He said, "Didn't you know that I must be in my Father's house?" (Luke 2:49).

We have often taken his words to be a pious statement by a precocious child. When Sunday school teachers told us this story, they pointed out that Jesus was far wiser than his years. At age twelve, he could hold his own with the brightest minds in Israel. And that is probably true.

But today I want to remind us that this is a story about a family under pressure. A mother and father were starting to lose their son. It's also a story of a child who was starting to listen for God's voice, rather than to the voice of his parents.

A family lived off the alley behind my first church. There were three floors to their row house, each floor inhabited by a different generation. The grandparents, who were members of the church, lived on the ground floor. Next floor up was their son and daughter-in-law, and the grandchildren's bedrooms were at the top.

One day, the grandfather beckoned me to the back fence. "I'm worried about my grandson," he said.

"What's the problem?" I asked.

He said, "When he gets up in the morning, he reads the Bible before he does anything else. Every time he sits at the kitchen table, he insists on saying grace. Now he's talking about joining a prayer group with his girlfriend."

"Walter," I said, "what's the problem?"

"Don't get me wrong, Reverend," he said. "Religion is a good thing, as long as it's in small doses. I'm worried my grandson is becoming an extremist."

I admit it was hard to sympathize with my neighbor. So far, no member of my family has been lost to such radical behavior. Neither has a child of mine wandered off to the Temple for three days. But it's important to remember that religious commitments can divide a family.

Dr. Stanley Hauerwas is a professor at Duke University. He often begins one of his college courses by reading a letter from a distressed father. The father is upset because his son has run off to join a weird religious group. He is writing to a government official, hoping for some kind of intervention. The religious group holds secret rituals at dawn. The leaders instruct the members to sell all worldly possessions and give away the proceeds. Group members insist on eating meals together, and the father is deeply disturbed about the influence of this group upon his son.

What's the name of this strange cult that snatched away the young man? The Christian church, circa 200 A.D.

Whose voice speaks louder? Your family's voice or God's voice? That is the issue for today, and it is not easily settled. As much as we prepare our children for independence, it is painful when they begin to claim it. As seriously as we nurture our children's faith, it can be unsettling when they begin to take faith seriously.

According to the Gospel of Luke, Jesus did not ease any such difficulty through his words or actions. One day he was busy teaching and healing. Someone announced, "Your mother and your brothers are here, but the crowd is so big they cannot get to you." But Jesus replied by using his family as a sermon illustration. "My mother and my brothers are those who hear the word of God and do it" (Luke 8:19-21). How do you think they felt when they heard his response?

After Jesus grew up, he made radical demands on anybody who wished to follow him. He expected disciples to leave their homes and families for the sake of the kingdom of God (Luke 18:29-30). He warned they would be betrayed and put to death by parents and brothers (Luke 21:16). And he insisted his disciples had to give their first allegiance to him. In the most radical words possible, Jesus said, "Whoever comes to me and does not hate father and mother, wife and children, brothers and sisters, yes, and even life itself, cannot be my disciple" (Luke 14:26). We are called to pursue a single-minded obedience to God that precedes all loyalties and obligations to our families.

And yet, Luke is clear that Jesus learned this obedience from Mary and Joseph (2:51). Thanks to them, his daily life was firmly rooted in the life and faith of Israel. The birth of Jesus, set within the context of world events, is also subject to obligations of the Torah. The child was circumcised, named, and dedicated, according to the Law of Moses. Growing up, it was his custom to attend the synagogue on the Sabbath day (4:16). As an adult, Jesus did not quickly dismiss the traditions of his family's faith, but drew upon them to nurture and strengthen his life. A few scholars have even suggested that Jesus came to Jerusalem for his Bar Mitzvah, and not only for the Passover holiday. We can't say for certain; but what could be more appropriate than for Jesus to sit in the presence of the rabbis, caught up in discussing the commandments of God?

At its heart, this story hints at the tension between two of those commandments. On the one hand, Mary and Joseph were justified in their anger. The law says, "Honor your father and mother." Putting your parents through three days of anguish is not a way to honor or respect them.

On the other hand, the young Jesus was pushing us beyond the horizon to a greater requirement of faith: "You shall love the Lord your God with all your heart, and with all your soul, and with all your might." For he said to them, "Didn't you know that I should be in my Father's house?" He was acknowledging that there is one family tie that transcends all bonds of biology and marriage. We belong to God even before we belong to our parents.

Even so, we live within families. God has intended that each one of us be raised within a caring and safe household. At its best, the family can be the smallest form of Christian community. We have an opportunity to learn love and trust from the people who are raising us, and an obligation to pass on that trust and love to them and others. As Frederick Buechner writes:

> *Our mothers, like our fathers, are to be honored, the Good Book says. But if Jesus is our guide, honoring them doesn't mean either idealizing or idolizing them. It means seeing them both for who they are and for who they are not. It means speaking the truth to them. It means the best way of repaying them for their love is*

45

to love God and our neighbor as faithfully and self-lessly as at their best our parents have tried to love us.[2]

We have aging parents and rebellious children, distant uncles and hovering grandmothers. What's more, lately we have had our share of noisy crowds and busy religious festivals. With the stress of the season, many normally loving relationships have become pushed to a breaking point.

With that in mind, following God's will is a matter of discernment. For Jesus, it meant a single-minded obedience that would send him to the cross, a commitment to God which would pierce his mother's soul (Luke 2:35). Perhaps that is the cross some of us are called to carry this Christmas: to stand up and testify to a God who guides our lives on a path that may stand at odds with our family's expectations.

For others of us, however, we may be called to express our love of God through a renewed love of family. There are fractured relationships to rebuild, long-broken ties to restore, ungracious relatives to whom we are called to speak a forgiving word. Today gives us an opportunity to strengthen our relationships to those people who have loved us, nurtured us, and set us free. A renewed commitment to our family may be one Christmas gift that is still waiting to be opened.

---

1. Laura Smit, "The Image of Home," *Theology Today* (October 1988), pp. 306-7.

2. Frederick Buechner, *Whistling in the Dark* (San Francisco: Harper and Row, 1993), pp. 81-82.

Light Of
The World

John 1:1-18

One of the striking features of the Gospel of John is the way it depicts the life and ministry of Jesus Christ. The other gospels usually tell us stories about Jesus. Then, like the disciples, we are left to ask, "Who is this, that wind and sea obey him? Who is this who feeds the multitude on a couple of loaves and a few fish?" But in the Gospel of John, there's never a doubt who Jesus is, because he tells us. Usually he does so with a statement that begins with the words, "I am." Put him in a situation and he will clarify who he is and what he has come to do.

You can put him in the desert surrounded by people who are chronically unsatisfied, and Jesus says, "I am the bread of life. Whoever comes to me will never be hungry, and whoever believes in me will never be thirsty" (John 6:35).

You can put him in the midst of people who are confused, people who ask, "Who are you, Jesus? What makes you different from all the other gurus, rabbis, and religious leaders?" And Jesus says, "I am the gate for the sheep. Whoever enters by me will be saved, and will come in and go out and find pasture" (10:7, 9). It is an act of self-definition.

You can put him at graveside, in the midst of grief-stricken people, and Jesus says, "I am the resurrection and the life. Those who believe in me, even though they die, will live" (11:25).

Or put him in the midst of people who feel disconnected by life's difficulties, and Jesus says, "I am the vine, you are the branches. Those who abide in me and I in them bear much fruit, because apart from me you can do nothing" (15:5).

In the Gospel of John, in one situation after another, Jesus defines himself and says, "This is who I am...." In the eighth chapter, Jesus says, "I am the light of the world. Whoever follows me will never walk in darkness but will have the light of life" (8:12). His words echo the opening words of the Fourth Gospel, where the writer defines the person and work of Jesus in terms of light. "What has come into being in him was life, and the life was the light of all people ... The true light, which enlightens everyone, was coming into the world" (1:3-4, 9).

Jesus says, "I am the light of the world." This is the kind of thing we might expect to hear in these days after Christmas. Not long ago we gathered on Christmas Eve to hear the prophet Isaiah say, "The people who walked in darkness have seen a great light." We don't know if old Isaiah had any idea who or what he was talking about, yet we celebrate Christmas as a festival of light. We string up twinkle lights on fir trees. We illumine our houses. We burn candles in the windows and plug in GE bulbs on the shrubbery. We burn up the kilowatts because Jesus Christ is born. In the bleak midwinter, why not shine a little light?

In fact, every Christmas in the church where I grew up, somebody always asked grown adults to dress up as shepherds and ushers to play the part of wise men. They recruited a young pregnant couple to take the role of Joseph and Mary. What about the baby Jesus? They could have gotten a real baby for the part, but it was always safer to hide a 100-watt light bulb in the manger, because, after all, Jesus Christ is the light of the world. We have heard him say it, although he never exactly said what that means. What can it mean for Jesus to say, "I am the light of the world"?

Elsewhere Jesus turns to the church and says, "You are the light of the world." Of course, that's the Gospel of Matthew, not John. And when he says it, he is specifically talking about doing good works. "All of you are a thousand points of light," he says, and then he adds, "Don't you dare hide your light under a bushel basket."

But here in the Gospel of John, Jesus never says, "You are the light." Rather he says, "I am the light." What does that mean?

You can sit in physics class and learn a lot of things about light. Ask Stephen Hawking, who holds the Newton chair at Cambridge.

48

He will tell you that light is the ultimate constant in the universe, that it always travels at 186,000 miles per second, that light transmits energy, radiation, and information. Or ask a third-grader to put a sunbeam through a prism and you will see the spectrum of a rainbow. Physics can tell us a great deal about light. But there's one thing physics has never explained, namely, what exactly do we mean by that word "light"? What is it? We know it when we see it, but we can't really explain what it is. Unlike space or time, light cannot be defined over against anything else. Light simply exists. What does it mean for Jesus to say, "I am the light of the world"?

Whatever it means, this is an important concept for the Gospel of John. Two different times, the writer depicts Jesus as saying, "I am the light." On many occasions, the writer affirms that the coming of Jesus into our world is not merely a light shining, but light breaking into the darkness. It is as if Creation is happening all over again.

For the writer says, "All things came into being through him, and without him not one thing came into being" (1:3). Look around a dark world and you may see it. The Creator of heaven and earth has come to visit his creation. Read the face of nature and it becomes obvious. See the snowflakes, so wondrously and specifically created. Look at the shadowy clouds, brooding with kindness. Listen to the chipmunk chattering on a tree limb. Watch the trout jumping for joy.

"All things came into being through him ... What has come into being in him was life, and the life was the light of all people" (1:3). That is, in Jesus of Nazareth, the very primal energy of the Creator is breaking anew not only in creation, but also in God's creatures. All of us were created in Jesus Christ. And all of us are re-created in Jesus Christ. "The true light, which enlightens everyone, was coming into the world" (1:9).

I begin to take seriously those words from the Christmas carol that says, "Light and life to all He brings."[1] See the freckled face of a child, re-created at 5 a.m. on Christmas morning. Or see it in the mischievous smirk of my grandmother. Last year she extracted her gleeful revenge on her once-loud grandson by giving a very noisy toy to his little girls.

For those who can see it, there is light and life given on Christmas. Ask the recovering alcoholic who finally gets through the holidays without needing a drink. Pay attention to the table where a stranger has been invited to fill an empty chair. See it in a sanctuary full of candles, "shepherds quaking at the sight," and tears streaming down the cheeks of bankers, bakers, and business people. Jesus said, "I am the light of the world." At Christmas time, we might not be able to explain completely the fullness of what that means, but we know it when we see it.

It's a new beginning, a new birth, for "Christ the Savior is born." And "to all who received him, who believed in his name, he gave power to become children of God," children re-born not through human means, but through the bright, shining grace of God (1:12). In that sense, Jesus is the light of the world. "Light and life to all he brings"; that's the promise for all who can believe it and embrace it.

And yet, I also need to warn you: Jesus is the light of the world. His light comes into our darkness. Let's admit that sometimes we don't want anybody to turn on the lights. There are deeds done in darkness that we don't want anybody to see. The coming of light means everything is exposed. Light means we have to deal with the truth. That can be very painful.

There was a priest in a midwestern city who wanted to help inner-city children. He wanted them to see something more than their own situations. He put them on a bus and took them to see some things of great beauty. They went to the art museum and saw paintings by the masters. They went to a symphony matinee and heard beautiful music. They went for a walk through a row of homes that were done over by a creative team of architects. That young priest showed those children the best and brightest things he knew. Then they climbed back on the bus and went home. That night one of those young boys set his apartment house on fire. They rescued the neighbors and family, but the place burned down. The priest was in tears when he visited the boy in a detention cell. "Why did you do it?" he asked.

"I saw all those beautiful things," said the boy, "and then I came home and saw how ugly my world was, and I hated the ugliness, so

I wanted to burn it down." Shine some light in a dark place and there's no telling what will happen.

When all you have ever seen is darkness, that is all you know. And when light comes, it makes for a contrast. Darkness remains a choice. In fact, it is possible for light to come into the world, and for somebody to say, "Turn out the lights!" It is possible for the Light of the world to shine on people, and those very people may not accept it. As someone once put it:

> *What is it to live in such darkness? We deceive ourselves if we think of primitive people in the dark remote areas of the world, still without digital watches and microwave ovens. We deceive ourselves if we think only of derelicts crawling along the dark alleyways of our cities. It is also darkness to refuse to hear the truth and to tolerate no teacher or preacher or politician who tells it. It is to avoid certain sections of town so as not to be disturbed by the conditions in which some have to live. It is to avoid any book or any speaker who shatters my illusions of innocence in this evil world. It is not to ask questions at work, at home, or at church because I prefer to let sleeping dogs lie. It is to persuade myself that problems in the schools, in the neighborhood, in society at large are really none of my business.*[2]

We know the darkness intimately. "This is the crisis of the world," says the Gospel of John. "Light has come into the world, and people loved darkness rather than light ..." (3:19).

And yet, the light of the world has come, and it is Jesus. Not just any light, but the light of the One who "brings grace and truth." He reveals the truth of who we are and who we are not. He also shines forth the grace of a God who gives life and rebirth. His truth is a light that exposes and reveals. But his grace is a light that renews as well as reveals, exposes and yet also forgives. The light is more than a candle in the night. The light of the world is Jesus, our Savior.

A friend named Tom tells about a night when he was a teenager. He and his friends were walking around the neighborhood. It was a warm night and very dark. Suddenly one of them saw a police car and shouted. They hadn't done anything wrong, but they didn't want to be seen, either. So they began to run. The police car saw them and watched them turn down an alley. Tom tripped and knocked over some trashcans. The police officers got out the car and began to go after them. One of the officers turned on a searchlight. Tom looked around for his friends, but didn't see them. All he saw was that burning, searing searchlight, looking for him.

Tom jumped behind those trashcans, only to find his friends huddled there. With frantic energy they tried to hide, pulling trash over their heads and hoping to blend in. The spotlight fell on Tom. "Come out where we can see you," said the voice behind the light. Tom stood up where he was, covered in garbage.

"What are you doing?" said the voice.

Tom stammered, "Nothing."

The voice said, "I can't hear you. What are you doing?"

Tom said, "Officer, I wasn't doing anything wrong; I saw the light, I ran, I knocked over these garbage cans. I'm sorry about the disturbance." The searchlight was beaming into his eyes, blinding him. He stood there in the light with nowhere to hide.

Then the voice said, "I think I recognize you. Don't you live around the corner?"

"Yes," he stammered. His heart was racing, and he thought to himself, "My life is ruined. If I don't get arrested for disturbing the peace, something worse will happen: this officer is going to tell my parents."

But then the voice behind the light said something unexpected. *"Son, I'm not here to punish you; I'm here to protect you."*

As he stood before that searchlight, Tom says he caught a glimpse of what it means to stand before Jesus, who is the Light of the World. There he was, fully exposed yet completely protected. He was fully revealed, yet free from unnecessary punishment. He stood hip-deep in garbage, yet cleaner than he had ever felt, somehow cleansed by a light that cast no shadow.

In that moment, he saw something of what it means to stand in the presence of Jesus Christ, who is full of truth and full of grace.

"I am the light of the world," says Jesus. "Whoever follows me will never walk in darkness but will have the light of life" (8:12). And the church affirms, "The light shines in the darkness, and no darkness shall overcome it" (1:5).

So brothers and sisters, I have only one thing to add: don't be afraid.

---

1. "Hark! The Herald Angels Sing," Charles Wesley, third stanza.

2. Fred B. Craddock, *John* (Atlanta: John Knox Press, 1982), p. 64.

What A Star Can't Tell You

Matthew 2:1-12

"Hi, Pastor! How are you?" She waved a glove from the other end of the parking lot. Pushing her shopping cart back to the front entrance of the supermarket, she wore a red parka from L. L. Bean. Her hair was pulled back in a hair band and her cheeks were flushed.

"I'm sorry I haven't been to church this winter," she said. "I bought a ski pass, and the lines are the shortest on Sunday morning."

I stood there with an artificial smile, trying my best to look cheerful. One of the frustrations of being a pastor who does not have free weekends is that I have to contend with those who do. "You ought to see the view from the top of that mountain," she said, inadvertently rubbing it in. "It's beautiful up there. Peaceful, too."

Then she said the line I've heard a hundred times. "To tell you the truth, Reverend, I feel much closer to God up on that mountain than I usually do in church."

I confess I never really know how to respond when somebody says something like that. I love the outdoors as much as anybody else does. There is nothing more enjoyable than a quiet getaway in the wilderness. Nobody knows more than me that the church can be a busy, uptight place where it's difficult to relax, much less experience the presence of God. As one overworked volunteer admitted, "Whenever I go to church, I always end up agreeing to do something. Sometimes I stay home on Sunday because, frankly, I need a break."

And yet something doesn't seem quite right when someone says they feel closer to God *out there* than they do *in here.*

For some, it may be a cop-out. If you're looking for good reasons to skip worship, there are plenty: college football games in the fall, winter sports in the winter, spring getaways, and summer vacations. Even some of our "regulars" will slip out of town at Christmas and Easter. As North Americans we live in a leisure culture, and there are many entertaining reasons why people don't go to church. The old starched Calvinist in me murmurs, "If worship was really important to these people, they would readjust their lives to attend." I realize my skewed point of view; I'm a minister, after all. But I am also a Christian. Whenever I miss worship on Sunday, it feels like I've jumped over an important part of my routine, like skipping a shower. Even worse, the accumulated grime does not get washed away.

Like I said, I might be the strange one. So this morning, I want to take seriously what she said. She said, "I feel closer to God up on that mountain than I do in church."

What she was saying is that nature can reveal the presence of God. It is possible to take a walk on the beach, climb a mountain, or swat a golf ball, and end up speaking a prayer of adoration. God has given us a beautiful world. There is no desert so desolate that you do not see God's fingerprints from creating it. Beyond the world, there are solar systems of intricate design and stars still uncharted. The immense size of creation can invoke awe, and turn us toward the intelligent Creator who made it.

That is what prompts the familiar story of the Wise Men. The magi search for Jesus because they have seen a sign in the world *out there*. An unusual star appears in the sky, and it causes them to recalculate their settled ideas about the universe. Clearly God is up to something, and the whole creation testifies to a new and wonderful act.

What is God doing? The Wise Men assume a new king has been born. In his commentary on the story, Raymond Brown observes that ancient historians often interpreted the skies through the births and deaths of famous people. The Roman historian Suetonius, for instance, claimed that the birth of Augustus was predicted by an unusual portent in the heavens. Emperor Nero became so alarmed when a comet appeared in the sky that he ordered the deaths of notable people in his realm.[1]

No one in the first century would have missed the connection between the unusual star and the birth of a significant new leader. But where was he born? To what royal family? Under what political circumstances? And what kind of king will he be? The magi cannot presume to know. Their knowledge is incomplete.

That is an important lesson to remember. As Garrison Keillor says somewhere, "If you get your guidance by following a star, the directions are going to be a little bit vague."[2]

For the past 400 years, we have turned to science to answer many questions. Scientists have analyzed the universe, discovered the laws of physics, studied the human body, and put bacteria under a microscope. We have learned a lot of things, many of them helpful and important. But there are still gaps in our knowledge.

You can learn a lot about the God who made everything, but you can't be sure what kind of God it is. There are sparkling waterfalls, bright autumn leaves, and radiant sunsets. But there are also black holes, mutating cancer cells, and raging storms that destroy without purpose. Look at the star in the sky and it's obvious that something is happening. But you aren't exactly certain what it is.

Many people have unusual experiences *out there,* and they don't know what to do with them. At a recent church conference, one of the most popular courses for adults was a class on interpreting dreams, near-death experiences, mystical phenomena, and topics that you might find addressed in the occult section of the local bookstore. A minister with conservative views on these topics heard about it and sought out the teacher. "Why are you teaching a class like this at a Christian gathering?"

The teacher said, "Look — a lot of people have questions about their own experiences. I am inviting them into my class so we can make some sense out of these things from the perspective of Christian faith."

I don't know how you feel about the appropriateness of that class, but I think the teacher's intention was right on target. A star can tell you that God is at work in the universe, but it cannot tell you where or how or why. And so, we bring our uninterpreted experiences of the world out there to the Scriptures that are kept in here. Then we listen to how the Scriptures read our experiences.

That is what the magi had to do. "We have seen a star out there in creation," they said, "and we believe a new king has been born somewhere." They go to the palace, because that is where kings normally come from. However the old king is still sitting on the throne and he isn't too excited about news of a new king.

Fortunately for the Wise Men, there are religious people on the old king's payroll, and they know what the Bible reported about the birth of Israel's new leader. The chief priests and scribes open up the scrolls to the fifth chapter of Micah and announce, "The new keeper of God's flock will be born in the city of David, who was the best shepherd we ever had."

Here is one glimpse of how we come to a deeper faith in God. We bring the things we have seen in the outside world into the sanctuary. In here, our experiences can be interpreted by a God who loves all people and works in the lives of exotic star worshipers. And if we follow God's direction, we will go in a different direction than bloodthirsty King Herod.

Even so, there is no assurance that knowledge of the Scriptures alone is sufficient for the worship of God. As someone writes:

> One can, like the chief priests and scribes, know the biblical facts but completely miss the deeper biblical truth. One can memorize verses, but forget the gospel. One can recite the kings of Israel and overlook the King of Creation. One can, like Herod, be in favor of studying the Scripture and still be on the wrong side of God's will.[3]

What's going on in the story of the Wise Men? On the one hand, the Wise Men arrive pondering the mysteries outside, discerning that God is up to something yet not certain where it might be happening. They need the Scriptures to clarify and confirm their search. On the other hand, the chief priests and scribes have the ancient scrolls at their disposal, but they are removed from the experience of awe that the Wise Men can claim. As a result, King Herod misdirects the information which he learns from the Scriptures and uses it to justify his terrorist schemes.

True worship brings together experience and Scripture. Mature faith requires awe from the world *out there* and knowledge of the God whom we worship *in here*. Herod has access to the Scripture, but he is unable to bend his knees in worship. So he orders a massacre.

The Wise Men, however, have seen the wondrous star. As they come full of awe, their believing hearts are informed by a Word from beyond their own experience. When they discover the child, "they knelt down and worshiped him. Then, opening their treasure chests, they offered him gifts of gold, frankincense, and myrrh" (2:11).

Here is something to say when someone announces that she prefers to worship God on the ski slopes. Out there in nature, there is no doubt the heavens are telling the glory of God. "Day to day pours forth speech, and night to night declares knowledge." Yet if you listen, you cannot tell what kind of God has made the world and the skies above. From nature alone, you cannot know much about the God who made the mountain and covered it with snow. If you fall down the slope and break your legs, you have no clue about the presence of the Creator. In the words of the psalmist, "There is no speech, nor are there words; their voice is not heard" (Psalm 19:1-3).[4]

So what do we do? We come inside the sanctuary to worship God. As we know, God made this wonderful creation and set the stars in the sky. We come in here to sing the songs and tell the sacred story. And we worship a God who loves us so much that he has given us Jesus Christ, the King of kings.

A star can't tell you that you are cherished by God. But the church can.

---

1. Raymond E. Brown, *The Birth of the Messiah* (New York: Doubleday, 1977), pp. 170-171.

2. From one of Keillor's unpublished Lake Wobegon monologues, broadcast on National Public Radio. Mr. Keillor is particularly fond of the magi, and they appear frequently in his Christmas stories.

3. Thomas G. Long, *Matthew* (Louisville: Westminster John Knox, 1997), p. 19.

4. Thanks again to Tom Long, whose exegesis and proclamation of Psalm 19 has informed my interpretation of the text.

Splashed With
The Spirit

Luke 3:15-17, 21-22

One Saturday when I was seventeen or eighteen, I had
an unusual religious experience. I was serving on my church's board
of deacons, and one of the middle-aged members of the board was
driving me around so we could drop in and visit some older members of our church.

This was during the late seventies, at a time when our congregation was going through some turmoil. A number of people had
been caught up in the charismatic movement that was going through
a number of churches. They started a Sunday night praise service,
sang Scripture songs, and prayed with their hands in the air. The
deacon who was driving me around that day was very involved in
the movement.

So there we were, driving around the countryside, supposedly
visiting shut-ins. We turned down an unmarked dirt road, and to a
little house sitting right on the edge of the road. My driver parked
the car, and we got out and knocked on the door. An old man opened
the door. His face lit up when he saw my companion and he stretched
up to hug his visitor.

Then my companion introduced me, and said something like,
"This is Bill. He's a good kid, and he is a deacon in our church. I
thought we could come in and talk with you. And then, maybe you
could baptize him with the Holy Spirit."

It made me nervous to hear him say it. I thought the man was
a shut-in. Actually he was a retired Pentecostal minister who had a
house church, which met in his small cottage. From what I could
tell, some people in our church were sneaking over to spend time

with him, because they felt they were getting something from him that they weren't getting from the Presbyterians. And now I had been taken to the hut of Brother whatever-his-name, in the hope that I would get whatever my driver and others had gotten from him.

I don't remember what we talked about. But I do remember, at one point, this old gnome telling me to kneel. Then he hobbled over, put his hairy hands on my forehead, and began to speak in a kind of mumble-jumble. This, it was later explained to me, was the gift of tongues. Suddenly he switched back to English and said in a loud voice, "God, I want you to baptize this dear boy with the Holy Spirit." And I tell you the truth: nothing happened.

I did not feel a warm fuzzy presence. I did not instantly understand all the mysteries of the universe. I did not speak in unknown languages. Nothing happened.

This troubled our host. He pressed down harder and spoke even louder. He said, "Lord, I insist that you baptize this boy with the Holy Spirit." Again, nothing happened. So the old man tried one more time, to no avail.

Finally the man who had brought me there spoke up and said, "Well, maybe Bill already has the Holy Spirit, and we didn't know about it." This was a new thought for our host, who stepped back and shook his head. Then I was helped to my feet, ushered out the door, and taken home.

Until this moment, I have never told anybody that story. Frankly I don't know what to make of it. It was a strange experience.

On the one hand, I did not know what he was talking about. When I was a little baby, a Presbyterian minister in Ohio splashed some water on my head and said, "You are God's beloved child. You have the Holy Spirit."

A dozen or so years later, I knelt with my confirmation class. Another minister said, "Your baptism is confirmed and you are a member of Christ's church. You have the Holy Spirit."

About five years after that, I knelt at the feet of a minister, and elders laid hands on me. They said, "You are ordained as a deacon in the Presbyterian Church. You have the Holy Spirit." Even before I could understand the gift, people were announcing, "You have been baptized. You have the Holy Spirit."

On the other hand, that strange trip out in the country has occasionally gnawed at my self-confidence. Ever since, I have wanted to know what it means to be "baptized with the Holy Spirit." That's what I want to talk about today.

Even though I couldn't name it at the time, the old man and my chauffeur were implying that whatever religious experiences I had up to that point were insufficient. They were declaring that I was an incomplete Christian, an unfinished disciple. As far as it goes, they were correct. Who among us is not incomplete and unfinished?

At the same time, they also assumed that I lacked a particular one-time experience which, if I received it, would make me complete and finished. It seems now as if they were trying to force upon me a gift that only God could give. It never occurred to them that perhaps God had already given it.

Let's face it: as far as faith is concerned, some people are late bloomers. It takes a while for some people to gain understanding.

Will Willimon tells about a church gathering where people were taking turns giving testimonies about their religious experiences. One man stood and said, "I was a Methodist for 38 years before anybody told me about Jesus." Will said he scratched his head when he heard that. What the man probably should have said was, "I was a church member for 38 years before I really experienced my faith and began to live it." That is, he had a delayed response. He was a late bloomer.

The problem, Will said, was the man sounded so smug when he said it. He made it sound as if there was an instantaneous experience that washed away his past. Well, says Will, what about all those teachers who put up with him while he was growing up in Sunday school? What about all of those preachers who tried their best to speak the gospel to him? What about all those Christians who tried to tell him about Jesus? Will felt like saying, "Listen, pal, it's nice that your faith is coming together, but what do you think we've been trying to get through your thick head for the last 38 years?"[1]

Faith is a seed that needs to take root. It takes time and nourishment to grow. Faith does not mature overnight. There are many seasons along the way. We must be grateful for those occasions when everything comes together, when the fog lifts and understanding deepens. Thank God for those moments when it happens.

There's a jazz musician I know who told me that he recently got baptized a second time. "I needed to do it again," he said, "because the first time didn't mean very much." As it turns out, he had been wrestling with his faith for years. We began to play music together in churches. As we traveled back and forth to each place, we talked occasionally about Jesus Christ. That was a catalyst, he said, for getting baptized a second time this fall.

Now, let me say that I am uncomfortable with what he did. By definition, Christian baptism is a one-time practice. Baptism is when we initiate someone into the Christian community. We initiate someone only once. The first baptism is the only baptism that counts, whether we know it or not. The rest of our life is a response to that first event.

Yet there's also something about my friend's experience that I want to affirm. The seed of faith is blooming in him. The presence of God is real to him in a way that was not real before. He has the Holy Spirit. Otherwise, how could he grow in his faith like that?

Faith takes a while to grow. Who knows why Jesus waited until he was thirty years old to be baptized? There are a lot of years in his life that we don't know anything about. Why did he wait until thirty? Why not 21 or 45? Why thirty? We don't know.

We do know, however, that the timing was right in more ways than we realize. For the gospel writers, the baptism of Jesus did not mark his coming of age. Rather it was the turning of all the ages, the hinge of history, when old gave way to new. The world changed at the Jordan River. John the Baptist said as much: "I baptize you with water; but there's someone coming who is more powerful than me. And he will baptize you with the Holy Spirit and fire."

John stood hip-deep in the river, splashing everybody with water. When Jesus came, the heavens opened, the Voice spoke, and he was splashed with the Holy Spirit. God's reign intersected with human history. The kingdom broke in and continues to break in.

The Holy Spirit is the sign that things have changed. It is the promise that the kingdoms of this world are becoming the dominion of our Christ.

There are two kinds of baptism mentioned in the New Testament. One is baptism with water. The other is baptism with the Spirit. John baptized only with water. It was a pre-Christian baptism. The water intends to wash away the dirt from your soul, to clean up every act. This baptism tells people to get ready, in case the Messiah should ever come.

The other kind of baptism is Christian baptism, which is done not in the hope of a Messiah, but with the assurance the Messiah has come. So it is baptism done in the name of Jesus. This baptism is done with water, because Jesus was baptized with water. But it is also done with the Holy Spirit, which comes as a gift from God. The Spirit fell on Jesus at his baptism. The Spirit fell on the church after his death and resurrection. Baptism in Jesus' name is a baptism of the Holy Spirit. We are not talking about two events, but one. In the words of the Apostle Paul, we have "one Lord, one faith, one baptism" (Ephesians 4:5).

That is to say, you may have the Holy Spirit and you didn't know about it. But what does that mean?

Luke has something very specific in mind. He describes the presence of the Holy Spirit differently from other writers in the New Testament. For the Gospel of John, the Spirit is the Spirit of Truth, the very presence of Christ, who comforts the faithful and leads them into the truth. For the Apostle Paul, the Spirit gives gifts like love, joy, peace, and patience to sustain the lives of the faithful. But for Luke, the word that best describes the Holy Spirit is *power*. The Spirit is the power of God, leading us into ministry, pushing us beyond self-interest, and moving us beyond our comfort zones.

According to Luke, "Jesus, full of the Holy Spirit, returned from the Jordan and was led by the Spirit in the wilderness, where for forty days he was tempted by the devil." Jesus confronted evil, not at a point of weakness, but at the points of his strength, assisted by the power of God's Spirit. As the story continues:

> *Then Jesus,* filled with the power of the Spirit, *came to Nazareth, where he was brought up, and went to the synagogue on the Sabbath day, as was his custom ...*

He unrolled the scroll and found the place where it was written: "The Spirit of the Lord is upon me. *He has anointed me to bring good news to the poor. He has sent me to proclaim release to the captives and recovery of sight to the blind, to let the oppressed go free, to proclaim the year of the Lord's favor.*"

What does it mean to be baptized by the Holy Spirit? It means we are commissioned for ministry. We are called to do God's work. We are given sufficient power to do what we must, wherever we are needed. It means God gives us the strength to do what God requires of us ... which, if you ask me, is the essence of grace.

If all that happens at a baptism is some splashing with water, or the giving of a name, it is not enough to prepare us for the kingdom that God is making possible. We need the fiery power of God, the full force of the love of Christ. And we name this power, this force, as the Holy Spirit. The Spirit will push us into places we would not expect. The Spirit will give us power to proclaim what God is doing in Jesus Christ. The Spirit will protect us from the puny powers of this age.

A minister named Al was pursuing a doctoral degree in theology. He worked long hours on his dissertation, so many hours, in fact, that his children often entered the study to interrupt. "Daddy, can you come out and play?"

"Sorry, kids," he replied, "I have too much work to do."

"What are you working on, Daddy?"

Well, he couldn't really give the title of his dissertation, which was something like "the experiential dimension of the divine pneumatological reality." So he said, "I'm writing about experiences of the Holy Spirit."

They looked at him with blank faces and said, "What's that?"

One day Al and his family were sitting in church. They had not expected much that morning, he says. The pastor was soft-spoken and meek. He never said anything very clearly, but everybody liked him. This particular Sunday was different. The pastor stood up and preached a powerful sermon on racial equality. This was during the sixties, in the South, in a white, middle and upper class congregation. People sat transfixed as the preacher laid his career on the line, perhaps even laid his life on the line.

"The day is coming," he said, "when all God's children, white and black, will join hands in worship and service. And that day is upon us."

The congregation left in shock. People couldn't understand how their mild, housebroken preacher could suddenly have been filled with such fire. On the way home, it occurred to Al what had happened. "Kids," he said, "remember how sometimes I go up to my study to write about the Holy Spirit?"

One of the children said, "Yeah, but Daddy, what's the Holy Spirit all about?"

Al said, "We got a good picture today, in church."[2]

They saw the power of God, pushing us to a day when every hand shall join in mission, when every voice shall join in praising the Lord. It is no empty promise.

Why, that power was given to us right over there ... *at the baptismal font.*

---

1. William H. Willimon, *Pulpit Resource,* 23.1, p. 10.

2. I am grateful to Thomas G. Long for telling me this story.

And On The Third Day ...

John 2:1-11

The story of the wedding at Cana is one of the most famous stories in the Bible. It has been the basis of many sermons
and numerous misinterpretations. In fact, there are so many good
misinterpretations of the text, I am not sure which misinterpretation I like the best.

I recall hearing a sermon based on this text. The preacher said,
"In Cana, everybody was having a good time at the wedding ban-
quet. There was a lot of music and dancing. It was a hot day. People
got thirsty. They ran out of wine. Everybody began to get sad. But
Jesus didn't want that to happen. Rather, he wanted a celebration.
So *voila!* Jesus turned water into wine, and the party continued."

"After all," claimed the preacher, "Jesus loves a good party."

Now that's something most of us want to believe. It is good to
think the Lord intends to bless our human celebrations. We hope
for the coming day where there will be a wedding feast of the Lamb
that never draws to a close. But as pleasant as the hope can be, it
has nothing to do with this text. There's no hint at Cana that Jesus
is a party animal. If anything, he comes across as a stern figure
who was annoyed to be called away from his table.

Another interpretation of the story came from a Bible study
group. The group was talking about the wedding at Cana story, and
someone said, "I think it's a wonderful tale. Jesus overcame his
initial hesitation to do the right thing. Think of it: The bride and
groom must have been terribly embarrassed. The party had gotten
out of hand. They didn't have enough hors d'ouevres. The roast
beef wasn't sliced thinly enough. Worst of all, the caterers ran out

of Zinfandel and Chablis. It must have been awful. But Jesus was there. He produced some wine, and everybody escaped what would have been a catering disaster!"

That, too, is an interesting view of the wedding at Cana. However, with all apologies to Martha Stewart, the Jesus portrayed in this text is not the least bit concerned about saving people from social miscues. He seems totally unconcerned about etiquette. Jesus took six stone jars normally used for Jewish purification rituals, and made them carafes of his new wine. Is Jesus concerned about social proprieties? I don't think so.

One Saturday in New England, a priest gave one more spin to the story. It happened at a wedding, of all places. The priest looked at the bride and groom and said, "You're about to begin a new life together. Sometimes this new life will fill you with joy and happiness. Other times, however, it may feel like you've run out of wine. When those dry occasions inevitably arrive, remember the wedding at Cana. Just turn to Jesus and ask him to fill you up with wine. He will always come to your assistance whenever you ask."

Of all the misinterpretations of Scripture I have ever heard, that misinterpretation is the most comforting. Unfortunately it can't be authorized by this text either. Jesus is at the party. The party runs out of wine. Nobody from the wedding party bothers to tell Jesus. It's just as well. When his mother brings up the matter, he essentially brushes her off.

She informs him, "They have no wine."

Jesus replies, "*Woman*, what concern is that to you and me?"

She looks at him with maternal pressure. He stares through her and says, "It's not my hour. It's not my time." Now, does that sound like a warm and supportive relationship? I don't think so. Jesus brushes off his mother's request. She backs off from her request, and *then* he makes the wine.

It is difficult to handle this story without it slipping out of our hands. It defies reduction. There is no simple application for our lives. So what is going on here? Is this a story about a wedding? I don't think so. This is a story about that uncommon wedding guest, Jesus Christ. And we have already heard three clues to understanding this story.

The first is this: Jesus uses a village feast, not as an opportunity to make people happy, but as an opportunity to reveal God. The writer says, "This was the first time Jesus revealed God's glory." Curiously, some people missed it entirely. Jesus stood before them with the power to turn water into wine. Those who really saw what happened could only comment on the quality of the wine.

The caterer was one of them. He thought somebody had pulled the same trick as a college fraternity I knew. Whenever the fraternity would throw a party, they would tell their guests to count on plenty of premium beer. In actuality they would buy only one case of the expensive brew, and after serving it to dull the taste buds of their guests, they tapped a vat of cheap ale. It was cheaper that way; and according to the second chapter of John, it is a long-standing practice.

"You have waited to serve the best until now." The caterer missed the point. But can you blame him? Jesus has revealed the glory of God, not in high and lofty places, but in the middle of a wedding. He revealed the presence of God, not in the reverent hush of a wedding performed in a sanctuary, but in the neighborhood bash immediately following. God drew near, amid loud music, the droning of distant relatives, and a three-tiered cake with plastic figures on top. It happened in such an ordinary place.

It reminds me of something Will Willimon once said. "Most preachers," said Willimon, "get it all wrong at weddings. They stand up and talk about *agape*, the love of God that descends from above. The bride and groom, on the other hand, are drooling in anticipation of *eros*, the earthy love that they can't wait to express."[1] Willimon is onto something. The glory of God is revealed in a very common human occasion.

After all, that's the central theme of the Gospel of John. Where do we find the fullness of God's glory? Not in the dead rituals or lofty traditions of organized religion, but in a specific human person, Jesus of Nazareth. The eternal Word becomes flesh. Knowing this does more than make people happy. It satisfies the deepest longings of the human heart.

That brings us to a second clue to the story's meaning. If the human Jesus is to reveal the everlasting God, some established

71

customs are broken. At Cana, Jesus used six large stone jars as carafes for new wine. Those jars were normally filled with water for purification ceremonies, for the ritual cleansing of dirty Jewish hands. Jesus claimed the authority to break the rules, and put those jars to another use. For those who knew what he was doing, it was disturbing, to say the least.

Imagine if a church member threw a party in fellowship hall. While the crystal punch bowl is carried down the steps, it accidentally slips and smashes on the floor. Uncle Joe says, "Don't panic. I know something we can use." He goes up the stairs into the sanctuary, hoists the baptismal font over one shoulder, and carries it down to fellowship hall. Then the caterers fill it with Canada Dry and cranberry juice. The font becomes a punch bowl. Get the picture? It's disruptive ... like what Jesus did behind the scenes at the wedding in Cana.

It goes to show there's no telling what rules Jesus Christ will break, in order to disclose the presence and power of God. All we can be sure is God's glory will not be reduced to traditions and rituals. According to the Fourth Gospel, Jesus Christ is not interested in maintaining stale religious customs and established patterns. Rather he is concerned with bringing us into the presence of the eternal God.

If you read the Gospel of John, you get the clear impression that whatever happened in Cana can happen anywhere, at any time. With Jesus around, every day is the third day. If we have eyes to perceive them, we see minor miracles every day, significant transformations that happen in your life or mine. They are no less far-reaching as what happened that day in Cana. When such a moment happens, the actual event is significant, but it's nowhere as important as what happens to us in the midst of the event. A sign from heaven can redirect you, turn you around, prompt you to participate in God's timetable for the world, where every day is the third day, and Christ's holy presence is with us.

Even so, maybe you know how disruptive it can be. One of the things God has been teaching me is that if we are to become new creations in Christ, we have to let go of the old patterns, the familiar ways, and the comfortable habits. That's not easy. The work of

Jesus Christ in our lives is always about making something new: beginning over, establishing new relationships, claiming a new start. Changes can be disruptive. They demand all the strength and courage we can find. But if we are able to embrace what God is doing, we may find that some of the best wine has been saved until now.

All of this points us to the third clue, that third insight into the story, namely, when new life comes, when the new wine is poured, it is the gift of Jesus Christ. He alone chooses to give the new wine. No one can force him to give it, not even his own mother. No one can tell him what to do. And when Jesus does choose to act, he does so entirely from his own initiative. Just recall a couple of the stories John tells.

One day, says John, the brothers of Jesus say, "Why don't you go up to Jerusalem? It's time for a public festival, and there everybody will see what wonderful things you do!"

Jesus replies, "No; my time has not yet come."

So his brothers go to the festival while Jesus stays behind. After his brothers depart, then Jesus goes to the festival too. He responds by not responding; then he responds, free from all their suggestions. Jesus doesn't need his brothers to tell him what to do. He already knows.

On another occasion, a multitude of people gathers around Jesus once they have heard how he can heal the sick. They are hungry. And Jesus asks Philip, "How are we going to feed these people?"

Philip says, "I don't have the slightest idea!"

The writer of John says Jesus asks Philip that question, even though Jesus already knew what he was going to do. He had already decided to feed the crowd.

On another occasion some messengers came to Jesus. They said, "Your friend Lazarus, the brother of Mary and Martha, is sick. He's near death!" Now, says John, Jesus loved Mary, Martha, and Lazarus. He truly loved them. So what does he choose to do? Well, when Jesus hears that Lazarus is sick, he stays two days longer in the place where he was. Then and only then he sets out for the tomb to raise Lazarus from the dead.

In the Gospel of John, no one can tell Jesus what to do. He never acts spontaneously. He is never surprised. He is never caught off-guard. He never improvises for the occasion. By contrast, he always acts intentionally and deliberately, for he is the Lord. He comes to show us what God is like.

As someone notes:

> In John's Gospel, Jesus speaks and acts not in response to any claims of kinship, friendship, or even need, but at his own initiative as God's will is revealed to him. This may seem to be without compassion, but something more than compassion is involved. In the Cana story as well as those involving his brothers and his friends, Jesus meets the need but he does more. Compassion alone might provide wine, but sovereign grace does more: it reveals God in what is done.[2]

On the third day, Jesus turned water into wine. On the third day, Jesus rose from the dead. And if every day is the third day, there's no telling what the Risen Christ might do among you and me, as he comes in the wild, unpredictable grace of God.

---

1. William H. Willimon, "June Weddings," *On a Wild and Windy Mountain* (Nashville: Abingdon Press, 1984), pp. 116-117.

2. Fred B. Craddock, et.al., *Preaching the New Common Lectionary, Year C, Advent-Epiphany* (Nashville: Abingdon Press, 1987), p. 130.

Today

Luke 4:14-21

In one of his books, David Buttrick tells about a cartoon in a magazine. The cartoon showed three men sitting in a row behind a long table. A microphone has been placed in front of each of them. One man was pictured in long flowing hair and a draped white robe. Another was battered, a wreath of jagged thorns on his head. The third was swarthy, with dark curly hair and a pointed nose. The caption said, "Will the real Jesus Christ please stand?"[1]

Everybody sees Jesus from a different angle, including the writers of the New Testament. For Matthew, Jesus is the Teacher of Righteousness. Like Moses, he climbs a mountain and teaches a new Law to his disciples. After Easter, he gathers them on a mountain and gives them a great commission, namely: to follow his teachings.

For the Gospel of Mark, Jesus is an exorcist, constantly battling the powers of evil. Even after Evil nails him to a cross, Jesus emerges from the tomb to continue his saving work. He is the Strong Son of God turned loose in the world.

According to the Gospel of John, Jesus comes to reveal God. "No one has ever seen God. It is God the only Son, who is close to the Father's heart, who has made God known" (John 1:18).

But for the writer of Luke's Gospel, the word that best summarizes the person and work of Jesus is the word "prophet." Jesus is a prophet.

What comes to your mind with the word "prophet"? Do you see a fortune teller? Or the seer who gazes into a crystal ball and predicts Super Bowl scores?

As the new century has dawned on us, I have kept my eyes peeled for a person with shaggy hair who walks down Broadway wearing a sandwich-board and screaming, "Repent for your sins! The End is near!" A lot of people think that's what a prophet should do: shout at people and make them nervous. As an old-fashioned radio preacher once claimed, "The truest test of prophecy is this: A prophet predicts doom of the sinner."

In the story we heard today, Jesus is a different kind of prophet. He stands squarely within the tradition of the prophets of Israel. In place of the sandwich board, Jesus wears a prayer shawl. Instead of screaming angry threats, he reads Scripture. Rather than standing on the fringe of the community, Jesus sits in the middle of the synagogue, the traditional posture of a preacher. There isn't the slightest hint that his eyes are wild or his hair is shaggy. He issues no burning cry for repentance, nor does he burden people with guilt.

According to the writings of Luke, Jesus is rooted in the faith of Israel. Luke alone says Jesus was circumcised on the eighth day. He reports that Mary and Joseph dedicated the infant Jesus in the Temple of Jerusalem. At age twelve, he celebrated Passover in Jerusalem with his family. As an adult, he worships in the synagogue on the Sabbath. When it was his turn to read the Scriptures, he was so well-versed in the Bible that he can find his place without using a table of contents.

Nevertheless, Luke says Jesus was a prophet. His role had nothing to do with his appearance. It had little to do with his familiarity with the traditions of Israel. Rather it had everything to do with his sense of *timing*. The prophet Jesus says, "Today this scripture has been fulfilled in your hearing."

That is striking. Jesus could have said, "Yesterday," as in, "Yesterday, this scripture was fulfilled." Looking backward holds some appeal for us. To believe in God is, in part, an act of memory. We recall everything God has ever done. We remember the creation of the world and the Garden of Eden. We remember getting out of slavery in Egypt, crossing the Red Sea, and entering the promised land. We remember Jerusalem, and Babylon, and returning home to Jerusalem. We remember Bethlehem, Golgotha, and the empty tomb. "If I forget you, let my right hand wither! Let my tongue cleave to the roof of my mouth" (Psalm 137:5).

Remembering is an act of faith. This is no idyllic memory of "good old days" that never existed. Look back, and you can see where God's hand has guided us over the years. Our memories can comfort us. "Yesterday" is a secure place to stand.

It's easy to live in the past. All of us do it, even preachers. I have a friend who is a minister. She is a wonderful storyteller. But there's one curious thing about her. The only stories she tells come from her college days. If she wants to speak about love, she tells a story about her first boyfriend in college. If she wants to talk about temptation, she speaks of dormitory parties. If she wants to preach about discovering God's purpose for her life, she speaks about discerning God's will during midterms in chemistry class.

One day somebody asked, "Preacher, why do you tell stories about college?"

She thought about it for a minute and said, "I guess those were the days when I felt most alive. Back in college, I felt very close to God."

"But, Preacher, that was twenty years ago. Has God done anything for you since then?"

It is a comfort to live in the past. But that's not what the prophet Jesus said when he spoke in the synagogue. He did not say, "Yesterday the scriptures were fulfilled."

Neither did Jesus say, "Tomorrow." Maybe we thought he would say, "*Tomorrow* the scripture will be fulfilled." Or at least he could have said, "*Someday* the scriptures will be fulfilled." An announcement like that could move our hearts toward hope. It could give us something to anticipate.

Twenty centuries have come and gone, and the world is still a mess. We know it. We wait for God to do something. As someone reminds us, it is no wonder that, in the time of Jesus, all the wonderful stories people told began not with "Once upon a time," but with the words, "When the Messiah comes ..."

- See a beggar on the street, hollow eyes gazing over an empty cup. "I'm sorry, friend, but someday, when the Messiah comes ..."
- To every crippled person, with twisted limbs folded beneath him. "I'm sorry, friend, but someday, when the Messiah comes ..."
- To every prisoner straining after a ray of light in the narrow window. "I'm sorry, but someday, when the Messiah comes ..."
- To every parent consoling a daughter assaulted by a Roman soldier. "Now, now, child, someday, when the Messiah comes ..."[2]

Looking ahead can become a way to live, a way to put our problems in perspective. Every time we see misery, injustice, and poverty, we can say, "Someday God is going to straighten this out. The day is coming when God will set everything right." Just say the word "tomorrow" over and over again. It can galvanize your hope and strengthen your resolve. It can also buy a little time.

One day, a wife said to her husband, "Honey, when are you going to wash those dirty dishes?"

"Oh, don't worry. I'll get to them a little later."

She said, "*When* will you get to them?"

He said, "Probably later this afternoon. Or maybe tonight. Or perhaps next Tuesday. I'm not sure; but don't worry. Someday I will wash those dishes."

Lazy husbands will tell you: You can get a lot of mileage out of that word "someday."

The people wanted to know, "Jesus, when will God scrub up our dirty world?" I suppose Jesus could have said, "Someday the Kingdom will come." He could have said that, but he didn't.

No, he went into the synagogue instead. It was the same familiar worship service. He looked around the congregation and saw the same faces. He stood and opened the Scriptures from the familiar scroll. He found his place in the sixty-first chapter of the prophet Isaiah and read the words, "The Spirit of the Lord is upon me ... to proclaim the favor of God." They were the same old words from Isaiah, which announced the same old hopes for the future. Everything was familiar and predictable.

But then, the prophet Jesus hurled a Word that shattered the status quo. The word he said was not "yesterday," and the word was not "tomorrow." The word was "today." Jesus said, "This is the day. The time has come. Today the scriptures are fulfilled."

I pause to remind us that "today" can be a dangerous word. It is the kind of word which creates hatred and opposition. A lot of people refuse to accept "today" as the day for anything. The chief reason? Because it reminds people of what they already know. That's dangerous!

When Martin Luther King, Jr., came preaching to the people in our country, he did not say anything new. His message was 200 years old: "We hold it to be self-evident, that all people are created equal." Dr. King looked out and saw people who were not treated as equals. He perceived others for whom this truth was not self-evident. So he went from city to city and said, "Today is the day when we will take seriously our own Declaration of Independence." Gunshots rang out and cut him down. Why? What radical act did he commit which took his life? In the tradition of the Bible's prophets, he reminded people of what they already knew and said, "Today is the day."

It is risky to stand up and speak of God in the present tense. When the prophet Jesus said, "Today the scripture is fulfilled," he turned memory into a mission statement. He transformed hope into an assignment. He claimed the beautiful poetry of Isaiah as his job description.

But the question remains: Is today the day? Is this day *really* the day?

Jesus said, "I have come to preach good news to the poor." Well, that is a noble thought, but what about us? The poor don't live on our streets. They don't move in our circles of friends. Even if they did, what kind of good news would we say to them? It is far easier to feed them from a distance, and send a few dented cans of creamed corn from the food pantry. Instead of getting involved, it is possible to perform a small deed to ease the conscience and avoid talking face-to-face. You never know when the dust of poverty may rub off on one of us ...

Jesus said, "I have come to proclaim release to the captives." That is another difficult assignment, because it involves speaking to those in captivity. Some of them are imprisoned behind bars. To proclaim release means to go where they are, and to speak a word that their jailers will not appreciate. Still others are captives in another way, confined by forces such as prejudice or sin. It will not be easy to announce their freedom.

And Jesus said, "I have come to proclaim new sight for the blind." Tell me: Do mere words have that kind of power? Can words help people to recover their vision? Can words remove cataracts or focus one's sight? We are only talking about words. What can words do?

And Jesus said, "I have come to liberate the oppressed." Wait a minute! That sounds so political. With every oppressed person, there is an oppressor. For every person who is held down or held back, there is somebody else who is doing the holding. Do we want to get tangled up in setting free the victims and the underdogs? That can be messy work. There are some respectable people we know who could be exposed as oppressors. If we get involved, we might lose friends and make enemies. It is far easier to play it safe and hide out in a comfortable church.

Jesus said, "I have come to proclaim the year of God's favor." Why, that may be the most difficult task of all. Imagine it: announcing all people are valued by God — *not* because of what they do, *not* because of where they live, *not* because of how much they earn, and *not* because of the level of their religious activity — they are valued because God is delighted with them. That may be the most difficult announcement a prophet ever makes. Who is going to believe it? The people to whom we are sent are more accustomed to measuring themselves by the world's yardstick and earning their own way. Jesus comes to people who don't ever feel like they measure up, and he announces to them the unrestricted acceptance of God. A lot of people cannot perceive the breadth of such mercy. How can anybody say, "This is the year of God's favor"?

I do not know, except to announce that Jesus said, "Today is the day." Check the calendar: not last Thursday, not next Tuesday. Jesus said, "Today is the time of God."

And he was right.

For anybody who would follow the prophet of Galilee, for anybody who would bear the name of "Christian," this is the acceptable time to share the love and justice of God.

Today is the day. Do you believe that?

---

1. David Buttrick, *Preaching Jesus Christ* (Philadelphia: Fortress Press, 1988), p. 23.

2. Fred B. Craddock, "Hoping or Postponing," *National Radio Pulpit,* 1978.

When The Sermon Turns Sour

Luke 4:21-30

I **want to** let you in on an industry secret. Ready? Most preachers have a difficult time preaching in the congregations where they grew up.

It is true for me. I was recently invited to preach in the church where I grew up. My mixed feelings about the invitation were justified. Before anybody heard a word I said, they remembered little Billy Carter, who made paper airplanes out of worship bulletins and dropped them from the balcony when nobody was looking. Even the newcomers who joined long after I moved away had been indoctrinated. They knew members of my family, and that became the filter through which they heard the content of my sermon. Before that congregation heard me, they already knew me.

So I can understand something of what is going on as Jesus returns home in this passage from the fourth chapter of Luke. He goes to Nazareth, his hometown (Luke underscores this point). No sooner does he read the Scriptures, and the murmurs are buzzing. "Isn't this Joseph's son? We know him. We like him. We expect him to be gracious and well-spoken."

It is difficult for a preacher to go back home. Everybody knows you. That is the problem. Of all the sayings of Jesus, one of the few things he said that appears in all four gospels is that a prophet gets no respect in a prophet's hometown.[1] Or to put it another way, "You become an expert only after you move more than ten miles from home."

It is possible to get too comfortable, particularly with the things that matter most. That's especially true for anybody who reads and

83

studies the Bible. In one of his books, Tom Long once made an astute observation about what often happens in the minister's study.

> *It is amazing how many of us, if someone were to ask us our view of biblical authority and inspiration, would articulate a dynamic view of the living and active biblical word. We would be full of ideas about how texts are always creatively engaging us with truths ever new. That is our official position, but in practice we look at a familiar text, like the "Prodigal Son," and we treat it as if it were a slightly senile dinner companion who tells the same story over and over again and never says anything new. We give the text a quick glance, maybe sneak a peek at a commentary or two just to make sure that what we have always thought that text was about is what it is about, and then stew about how to say the same old thing in some sparkling way.*[2]

The assumption, of course, is that this or any other Bible passage is the "same old thing," and that there is no power in the same, old thing. And so, you have to find something new in order to be heard.

When I began my work as a preacher, I spent a lot of time poking around the pages of Scripture for something unusual. My only objective was to find something that would prompt me to say, "This will get them." I would find something in the book of Obadiah and preach on it, murmuring, "I'll bet they have never heard this before." I was right; they had never heard it before. As a result, it had no power. No authority. No sense of importance or urgency.

Once in a while, I would give in and turn to a text that everybody had heard before. At coffee hour, folks would say, "Whew! You really gave it to us today!" Little by little, it began to dawn on me: The power of the prophetic word does not come from roaming a far country where no one has gone before. The real power of the gospel comes from reminding the people of God of what they already know.[3]

At a far deeper level, that's what happened in Nazareth that day. Jesus strolls into his hometown. And yes, everybody knew him. He takes the dusty scroll of Isaiah, finds his place, and reads, "The Spirit of the Lord is upon me, and has 'christened' me to bring good news." And everybody nods and says, "That's right! Preach the word!" So Jesus tells them two more stories out of their own Bible, a story about Elijah and a story about Elisha. Suddenly the crowd growls, curses him, and tries to hurl him over a cliff.

All Jesus did was to tell a couple of Bible stories that his listeners already knew. As a result, they wanted to murder him. Those who were most familiar with him turned against him, and wanted to put him to death.

No doubt, when the writer of the Gospel of Luke thinks about Jesus, he has the ancient prophets in mind, those unmanageable people who got up and spoke a Word from God. Luke is well aware that Jesus stands at the end of a long line of prophetic succession. And for him, that's the root of all the trouble.

According to the story, some friends feared for his safety. In chapter 13, they warn Jesus, "Stay away from the Holy City. Your life is in danger." But Jesus replies to them out of the side of his mouth: "I must go to Jerusalem, I absolutely must; because that's the city that always kills the prophets."

Not long after that, Jesus comes around the bend on Palm Sunday. He sees the city, stops dead in his tracks, and begins to weep. "Jerusalem, Jerusalem! If only you knew the things that make for peace. Instead you are too busy murdering the prophets."

Even on Easter: the news came out that Jesus was risen; but his own disciples didn't believe it. Jesus joins two of them on the road to Emmaus, but they do not recognize them. So as they walk, Jesus interprets the Bible. He reminds them of what the Good Book says. And it fills his disciples with heartburn.

Luke wants us to know that the most scandalous thing we can ever do is to hear the Bible. The most outrageous thing we can do is to take the Bible seriously, not only as a comforting word, but also as a deeply disturbing word. The main reason why it is so disturbing is that it reminds us that God does not play by our rules or stick to our boundaries.

Some of you have heard about Clarence Jordan, founder of Koinonia Farm in Georgia. He started a peanut farm and tried to run it the same way he thought Jesus would run it. He believed in a good wage for an honest day's work. He believed in taking care of the land and those who work it. And he believed that all people — black and white — could work together and stand together. It was the early 1950s, and his local Baptist church did not agree with his thoughts on racial equality.

One time, an agricultural student from Florida State University visited Koinonia Farm for the weekend. The student was from India, and said, "I've never gone to a Christian worship service. I would like to go." Clarence took him to Rehoboth Baptist Church, and it is reported that "the presence of his dark skin miraculously chilled the hot, humid southern Georgia atmosphere."[4] It didn't matter that he was from India. He had dark skin, not a red neck — and so he did not fit in.

After worship, the pastor drove out to Jordan's farm and said, "You can't come with somebody like that. It causes disunity in our church." Jordan tried to explain, but the pastor wasn't listening.

Sometime later, a group of church leaders went out to the farm to plead with Clarence to keep undesirable people out of their church. As the story goes, Clarence promised to apologize before the congregation if somebody could prove he had done something wrong. Then he handed a Bible to a man in the group and said, "Can you tell me what sin I have committed by bringing a stranger to church?"

The man slammed down the book and said, "Don't give me any of this Bible stuff!"

Clarence retorted, "I'm not giving you any Bible stuff. I'm asking you to give it to me."

The man and the others did not know what to say; so they slipped out. When they got back to the church, they wrote a letter and said, "Mr. Jordan, you are no longer welcome in our church, because you keep bringing in the wrong kind of people."

As one commentator notes, "Jesus is not acceptable in his own country because his mission extends beyond his own country."[5] Israel was called to be a light to the nations, a beacon of God's mercy for all people everywhere. When God's light began to shine in Jesus of Nazareth, it exposed dark crevasses everywhere, even in Israel. Some of the people slithered out of the dark and tried to snuff out the light.

It is much more comforting to believe that you have learned all you need to learn, to affirm that the way you have always done it before is a good way to keep on doing it. That is a satisfying way to ride through the whitewater of change. Just hang on and coast for a while. It works fairly well, until you realize that the way you always did it before may not have been the way it was always done.

Remember a few years ago? There was a piece in a national magazine about a scholar in a major university. After years of careful historical research, this shy professor discovered there was a period in the Middle Ages when the Roman Catholic Church approved of, and actually conducted, marriages between gay couples. He had the facts to prove it. And the Vatican tried to squelch his research in a hurry.

In Nazareth, a sermon turned sour. It started out sounding so familiar and comforting. And then Jesus raised a question: "How far is God's reach?" It was, and still is, a troubling issue. To think that the reach of God might far extend our own! To consider that the kind of people with whom God might choose to associate is different from our list. That is disturbing.

I worshiped one Sunday at a church in a seaside city in another state. The 11:00 service was jammed for something they called "Scottish Heritage Sunday." All the men were wearing plaid skirts. Some of the women were, too. I looked around that sun-tanned congregation while the bagpipes were playing. It was obvious from their appearance that most of those people in that congregation had gotten off their yachts, walked up the boulevard past all the specialty shops, and entered the church. They seemed so comfortable and settled. I, on the other hand, didn't feel for a minute like I fit in. And I sat there thinking, "Good thing there isn't a ghetto around here, or a Gay Pride parade on the street outside, or visitors from India — because people like that wouldn't be welcome."

Oh, I know — every church likes to paint a big sign and put it above the door: "We are a friendly church. Everybody is welcome." But when you go inside some churches, you realize it is reserved seating only.

Jesus looked at his Jewish congregation and said, "Let me tell you a Bible story. Remember Elijah? He was the greatest of all our prophets. And there was a famine in the land of Israel for three years and six months. Crops withered. The soil cracked. Not a drop of rain for years. And there were a lot of widows in the land of Israel in the time of Elijah. But remember where he went? God sent Elijah to a *Gentile* woman in Sidon."

"Let me tell you another story," Jesus said. "Remember Elisha? He followed Elijah, and whatever spirit Elijah had, well, Elisha was given a double share of it. He was a powerful man. And in his time, there were many people with leprosy in the land of Israel. They were sick and covered with sores. But Elisha didn't heal any of them. Instead he was sent to Na'aman, a *Gentile* army commander in Syria. And he healed the Gentile; he didn't heal any of the Jews."

When the Jewish people heard this, they were absolutely furious. It suddenly struck them what Jesus was really saying. He was declaring the disturbing news that God loves everybody, particularly those beyond their tight, exclusive circle. It was, and is, a scandalous thing to say.

The only thing more disturbing is to remember how that is the sort of thing that is written down in our Bibles.

---

1. As reported in Matthew 13:57, Mark 6:4, Luke 4:24, and John 4:44.

2. Thomas G. Long, *The Senses of Preaching* (Atlanta: John Knox Press, 1988), p. 31.

3. I am grateful to Dr. Fred B. Craddock for these insights.

4. The story is reported by Dallas Lee, *The Cotton Patch Evidence: The Story of Clarence Jordan and the Koinoia Farm Experiment* (New York: Harper and Row, 1971), pp. 75-76.

5. Luke Timothy Johnson, *Sacra Pagina: The Gospel of Luke* (Collegeville, Minn.: The Liturgical Press, 1991), p. 82.

The Kind Of People Whom God Chooses

Luke 5:1-11

There are many stories in the New Testament about people who are called to serve God and follow Jesus. Of all those stories, this story makes the most sense.

Remember the story about Paul? He was persecuting the church, dragging Christians out of their houses and condemning them to death. One day, he saw the Light, and it knocked him off his horse. It's hard to relate to such a dramatic conversion, but there it is.

Remember the story about Matthew? One day he was sitting at his tax collection table, minding his own business and counting the change. All of a sudden, Jesus looked at him, and said, "Get in step and follow me." Matthew didn't take time to think about it. He stood up and went. It is difficult to understand such an abrupt decision, but there it is.

Remember the story of Nathanael (John 1:43-51)? His brother Philip told him about Jesus. It sounded interesting, until Philip said, "And he's from Nazareth!"

Nathanael said, "Can anything good come out of that one-donkey town?"

Just then, Jesus said, "I saw you under a fig tree before Philip called you."

Suddenly Nathanael began to state a Christological formulation: "Rabbi, you are the Son of God, the King of Israel!" It is curious to hear about such instant orthodoxy, but there it is.

But the call of Simon Peter? That story is far more satisfying. The way Luke tells it, Simon wasn't sure that he fit into the whole Jesus business. It took some time for him to figure it out, and even then he had some misgivings. Did you hear what he said? "Get away from me, Lord. I'm not a good enough person for you." That's the way Luke tells it.

If you listen to the Gospels of Matthew or Mark, the story is much shorter. Jesus said, "Come, follow me!" Immediately Simon Peter dropped his net on the sand and off he went. No questions in his heart. No doubts in his mind. No inner conflict. No sense of inadequacy. Immediately he went.

But as Luke tells the story, it sounds like it could have happened to you or to me. By the time Jesus gets to the beach in chapter five, he has already been to Simon Peter's house. He went there after preaching a sermon one day. Simon's mother-in-law hadn't heard the sermon. She stayed home with a very high fever, and they asked Jesus about her. So Luke says he stood over her and screamed at the headache. The headache left her, so she got up and made some soup. Jesus went to that house long before he ever mentioned a job change to Simon Peter.

And there is no telling Simon would have taken it any way. Who wants a Boss who screams at your mother-in-law's headache?

Then Jesus went down to the lake to preach on the beach. It would have been a serene place to hear a sermon, but there was a crowd pressing up against him. So he climbed into Simon's boat, pushed out from shore, and began to speak some more. All of this happened before he said, "Come, follow me."

After Jesus finished speaking, they pushed themselves into really deep water. Jesus proved himself to be the first in a long line of preachers who could offer some advice on fishing. It didn't sound like good advice, and Simon said as much. But Jesus insisted. They threw in their nets and the catch was unbelievable! Fish began to swim into the nets and jump into the boat. There were so many fish, the boat began to sink with Jesus still in it.

Somebody whistled to shore: "Get another boat out here, so we can save the Savior." It was a silly thing to say.

For one thing, there were too many fish, and too little deck space. For another, a Savior doesn't need much saving. The other boat came out anyway. The fish began to jump into that boat. The boat began to sink. Next thing you know, all those men began to yell at one another: "Get these boats to shore."

Peter was on his knees, absolutely enshrouded in amazement. Then he said the first truly intelligent thing he said all day: *"Get away from me, Lord, for I am a sinful man!"*

If you ask me, that is a story that I can understand. It's not particularly dramatic, abrupt, or instant. Instead it is time consuming, unfinished, and it smells like a fish story. At a moment when Simon Peter the fisherman gets the catch of the century, he wants to push away the Founder of the Flounders.

And who can blame him?

The church has manufactured its own mythology about the first disciples. We have spun tales about their grounded faith and their perfect understanding. We want to believe that they had their collective act together. We want to affirm them as competent and capable, always knowing the correct answer to a question or the perfect solution to a problem.

But that was not the case. The twelve disciples were ordinary people, like you and me.

I don't know about you, but that makes me feel a whole lot better. Following Christ is difficult enough. It is an awesome task to live as God's person in a world like this.

It is even worse when you're a leader, under the scrutiny of the others, with demands put on you to lead God's rag-tag bunch. Who among us is qualified to lead, let alone follow? Who among us has enough holy traits, or few enough bad habits? Not one. According to the Bible, all kinds of people have said so.

Abraham said, "I'm too old."

Jeremiah said, "I'm too young."

Moses said, "I don't talk so good."

Mary said, "I am only a woman." God never hears any new excuses.

Simon Peter pulled in a load of fish, and said, "Lord, get out of here. I can't handle this. It is too much for me to take in. I am not the kind of person who can handle such generosity. I am not good enough to have you in my boat."

Call him, if you will, the patron saint of inadequacy. Simon Peter stands in a long biblical tradition.

These days, the church still squabbles about who is good enough to serve the Lord. When that happens, I suggest we read the Bible. None of us are good enough, but God wants us anyway.

That is not to say the work is easy. Jesus said, "I want to invite you to give up fish to go fishing." Ever since the time of Jeremiah,[1] whenever anybody talked about "going fishing," it was a metaphor for doing God's work. When Jesus said, "Go fish," he meant to gather in as many fish as we could, so that God alone can sort out the good and the bad, and ultimately God alone can decide what to keep and what to throw back.

For our part, we are called upon to throw out the net as far as we can, and then see what happens.

So the first word he speaks is: "Don't be afraid!" We can be amazed, painfully aware of all the problems we face and the limitations we know.

Yet he says to us, "Don't be afraid!" It is Christ's call, Christ's work, and Christ's miracle. The invitation doesn't begin or end with us. The One who calls us is the One who knows that he only has imperfect people to call. For our part, we simply have to decide if we are going to get out of the boat once we land on shore.

As Joseph Fitzmyer points out, when Simon says, "Go and leave me," Simon acknowledges that Jesus is rooted in "a realm or sphere to which he himself does not belong."[2] The One who calls us in the midst of our inadequacy is the One who ultimately judges us adequate. None of us are ever good enough, but God is good enough. And that's where we must start and finish.

The people who should scare us the most are the people who answer the call of Christ with such smug self-confidence that they know exactly what they are going to do. The person who thinks that she or he has all the answers frightens me. People like that are scary, because they follow their own agenda — and do not pursue what is most healthy for the whole body of Christ. A self-righteous servant is a contradiction in terms. The only person whom God can use — and by this I mean the *only* person — is the person who can hold humility in one hand, and in the other hand, confidence in the gospel which redeems us.

The invitation to serve and follow Christ is greater than any one of us can fulfill. When the invitation comes, we are called beyond our feelings of inadequacy to grow into the role, to claim the purpose, and to invest ourselves in Christ's future. It is a future when we will be presented, not in our own power, but in Christ's power, fully mature, fully humble, and full of love.

A number of years ago, Dr. John Hubbard, the former president of the University of Southern California, took a trip to Texas. While he was there, he met Tom Landry, the coach of the Dallas Cowboys. When he left, Coach Landry gave him a Dallas Cowboy t-shirt. Sometime later, Dr. Hubbard put on the shirt, and went out to play a round of golf. His caddy noticed the t-shirt and said, "Sir, are you the coach of the Dallas Cowboys?"

Without thinking, Dr. Hubbard said, "No, I'm not the coach. I guess I'm a scout."

The caddy was deeply impressed, and said, "I play football for Cerritos Junior College. Someday do you think I could play for the Cowboys?"

Dr. Hubbard sized him up and responded, "Son, I don't know if you have the size to play professional football. But keep at it, for you never know what might happen."

By the time he sank his final putt, Dr. Hubbard was feeling a little guilty about what he said, so he turned to the caddy and said, "I want you to have this t-shirt, but I'm afraid it is too big for you."

The young man smiled at him. Then he said something very wise. "Don't worry, sir. I'll wear it until it fits."

---

1. Jeremiah 16:16

2. Joseph A. Fitzmyer, *The Gospel According to Luke I-IX* (New York: Doubleday, 1981), p. 587.

Hated, Excluded, Reviled, Defamed — And Leaping For Joy

Luke 6:17-26

In a certain town, a man walked into a bookstore to return a purchase. "It's a Bible," he said, handing to the clerk at the cash register.

"Was it a gift?" asked the clerk.

"No, I bought it for myself," he said, "and I made a mistake."

"Didn't you like the translation? Or the format?"

"Oh no," the man said, "the format was clear and the translation was fine. I made a mistake."

The clerk said, "Well, I need to write down a reason for the return."

"In that case," said the man, "write down that there is a lot in that book which is tough to swallow."

There are some passages in the Bible that are tough to swallow. This is one of them. The burden on us is not to believe some astonishing miracle. There are events described in the Bible which stretch our credulity, moments which provoke us to scratch our heads in curiosity; but this text does not speak about any of them.

The burden on us is not to accept some rigorous demand. In many other places in Scripture, Jesus frequently demands that we do some actions that are difficult to do. Immediately after this passage, for instance, Jesus says, "Love your enemy." Elsewhere he challenges somebody to unload all of his possessions. Here he makes no such demand.

No, today's text is downright difficult to comprehend. The Lord describes the world in ways quite different from the ways we are accustomed to seeing it.

"Blessed are the poor, woe to the rich. Blessed are
the hungry, woe to those who stuff their stomachs.
Blessed are those who weep, woe to those who laugh.
Blessed are those who are hated, woe to those with a
good reputation."

What a strange way to look at reality! The ones whom the
world ignores are the ones who receive God's blessing. The ones
whom the world honors are the ones who are cursed. It is a complete reversal of the way we usually see things.

Passages like this can be found throughout the Bible. When
they appear, a lot of people, myself included, will do whatever
they can to soften them a bit and make them more applicable to the
world as we know it. As far as this passage goes, there have been
attempts to remove these words from the realities of every-day
life, perhaps even to lift them to a more exalted realm.

"Blessed are the poor," Jesus announces in the Gospel of Luke.
If you flip over to the Gospel of Matthew, you hear that pronounce-
ment turned into a spiritual virtue. "Blessed are the poor in spirit,"
says Matthew, revealing a different agenda at work. According to
Luke, there's nothing spiritual at stake; the blessed ones are merely
poor. Likewise, in the Sermon on the Mount, God blesses those
who are hungry for righteousness. Here God blesses those who are
hungry. We cannot spiritualize the circumstances or glamorize the
condition. Jesus means what he says: poor is poor, hungry means
hungry. And he announces both as "blessed."

As someone observes:

> *Jesus is making the official proclamation of the way*
> *life is inside and outside the reign of God. These are*
> *not suggestions about how to be happy or warnings*
> *lest one become miserable; blessings and woes as words*
> *of Jesus are to be heard with the assurance that they*
> *are God's word to us and that God's word is not empty.*[1]

Blessed are the poor. Blessed are those who are cursed for
Christ's sake. How are we going to cope with these words?

One suggestion might be to turn them into a strategy. It's not hard to do. You can put yourself under the blessing and change your circumstances so it applies to you. I have known people who are so hungry for the love of God that they will do almost anything to earn the blessing.

In college, I met a man named Stephen who claimed to be a "recovering Jew." He had been raised to keep his distance from Christians. Now, due to the meddling of God, he had become a Christian. And he was so much more zealous than I was.

He walked into my dormitory room one time and said, "I don't know how a brother in the Lord can own any jazz records. It's the Devil's music. We're having a bonfire this weekend. You're invited to bring those records ..."

I didn't like him. I tried to ignore him.

One day we were talking about the disciplines of the spiritual life. Stephen announced he had decided to fast. He intended to give up food and water for forty days and forty nights, just like Jesus. On day seven, he said, "I guess grapes might be okay." We watched him wither for another week.

Someone asked, "Why are you doing this?

Stephen replied, "The Bible says, 'Blessed are the hungry, for they will be filled.' So I'm making myself hungry so that God can fill me up."

It seems foolish, but some people would reduce these words to a strategy. We hear God bless the poor and say, "Now they are going to be rich. God will lift them up."

The problem with the scenario is that nobody ever gets ahead. God will lift up the lowly; the next day they will be exulted and acclaimed, so God will have to knock them down to size. It doesn't make any sense. If you are hungry, the day is coming when you shall sit and eat your fill. Later on, when you're full, God will knock you back down to size. That seems to be the logic of the passage, and it doesn't make sense.

Obviously we are not supposed to hear these words as a scientific formula. We cannot earn God's blessing. At best we can only hear it. It's for you or it's not for you.

And when I look at my bank account, meager as I think it is, and compare it to the income of the people in third world countries, and I hear Jesus say, "Woe to the rich," I realize he's pointing the finger at me.

If these blessings and woes present a strategy, it is God's strategy, not ours. That is why all of this is so tough to swallow. God refuses to leave the world in the same way *we* found it. God makes decisions and choices. God establishes a set of values. When you hear it, you have to decide, "Is God on my side, or is God on somebody else's side?" That's troubling.

Taken as they are, the blessings and the woes are perfectly matched — poor or rich, hungry or full, weeping or laughing, defamed or honored. For every blessing, there is an equal and opposite woe. Most of us would like to choose whether we will be blessed or cursed, but it's not our choice. It is God's decision. Sorry, but there's no sign-up sheet in the narthex.

It is hard to hear all of this, unless we hear it as an indication of God's agenda for human life. It's like one of those occasions in an African-American church when the sermon is long and the service even longer. Why are the people there?

They are there because if the preacher is on target, and the service is faithful to the gospel, they will break out in laughter. It is laughter over against the power of all the oppressors, and there's nothing anybody can do to squelch it.

It is difficult to hear the laughter if you're standing in the wrong place.

The point seems to be that God will win over all the forces that take away a person's humanity. That was the message of the sermon a few chapters before when Jesus preached in Nazareth. He read a section from the prophet Isaiah, "The Spirit of the Lord is upon me, because he has anointed me to bring good news to the poor. He has sent me to proclaim release to the captives and recovery of sight to the blind, to let the oppressed go free" (Luke 4:18). Jesus stood and said, "This is the day! God will win over poverty, captivity, blindness, and oppression." So as he heals here in chapter 6, he repeats that sermon all over again.

Perhaps the geographical location matters: Jesus is on level ground. He does not say these words from a mountain like a new Moses who lays down a new law with all authority in heaven and earth. No, according to Luke, Jesus stands on the flat land, among people who are sick and troubled. After a long day of curing every single person (Luke 6:19), Jesus fleshes out his deeds with his words. Somehow, in his very person, the acts of healing are held together with the words he speaks. They cannot be split apart; both testify that a new and redemptive day is at hand, promised in the person of Jesus.

Today is the day. "The poor are blessed. The hungry are filled. Whoever is cursed in my name will be given my name over theirs."

That's the clue to understanding these words and taking them in. Jesus is speaking to his own disciples, to anybody who hears these words and wishes to follow him. If you hear these words spoken to you, as an insider, you begin to see the world differently.

Here's the gospel truth: If God has embraced you, the world can't take that away. What people say about you doesn't matter compared to what God says about you in Jesus Christ. The world's neglect or mistreatment does not have to determine how you will live and act. When you are beaten up or put down, remember that in Christ there is a love that surrounds you and will not let you be snatched away. That is the good news for you and me. Thanks to Jesus, we belong to God. Nobody can cancel God's prior claim on our lives.

Who are you? Rich or poor? You are a child of God.

Who are you? Hungry or full? You belong to the covenant of Jesus Christ.

Are you all that people say about you, whisper about you, murmur about you? No, you have been baptized into the name of the Trinity, and no one can take that away. Blessed are you.

If you can swallow these words, it develops a different view on reality. Sometime before she died, someone had the audacity to ask Mother Teresa, "Why do you spend so much energy on the poor, the hungry, and the weeping of those in Calcutta?"

She respond, "Don't you believe the Bible? Jesus says the poor are the blessed ones. I take him at his word. I treat them as the royalty of God's kingdom, because they are."

To grow into becoming a Christian is, in no small part, to be converted into seeing the world as God sees it. It is to be given new eyes to look upon people and events from an eternally loving perspective. When that begins to happen, you begin to see that God has an opinion about how life should be lived, what churches should be doing, and how people should act. You begin to see that the future belongs to those whom God blesses. They include the poor, the hungry, the hopeless, the damaged, and those whose only salvation is found in the God who comes to redeem.

Around the time of the 1994 elections in South Africa, a friend was doing some academic research in that country. As you may remember, it was a difficult time in that nation. The country of South Africa was struggling to create a free society for people of different races.

One Sunday night, my friend drove into Pretoria, the administrative capital of South Africa. He describes it as an impressive city of steel and glass, with imposing government centers and modern universities. As he drove into the downtown area, he was stunned to see a small congregation of black Christians worshiping inside the green circle of an expressway ramp. He said:

> *The contrast could not have been more stark. Here against the skyline of the great governmental city of Pretoria, strong symbol for many of the bitter years of apartheid, was a tiny group of those who had been denied standing in the society. Here, in the shadow of the capital of a nation built on gold and diamonds and ivory, was a poor band of Christians with no building, no pews, no paid clergy, no musical instruments save tambourines ... Pretoria stood majestically, the embodiment of the present power. The little flock danced and sang and praised the God of Jesus Christ in the power of the Holy Spirit.*[2]

If the scene had been filmed on the evening news, the camera would have quickly passed over the worship service and panned the impressive skyline of the city. Anybody who knows anything about power would quickly affirm that the little congregation could easily be squashed by the imposing social order. Yet as my friend drove on, he found that his toes were tapping to the joyful songs of people who trusted in the God who makes all things right.

According to the regular order of things, those people are poor, hungry, defamed, and anonymous. But according to Jesus Christ, the future belongs to them.

---

1. Fred B. Craddock, *Luke* (Louisville: Westminster John Knox, 1990), p. 87.

2. Thomas G. Long, "Preaching God's Future: The Eschatological Context of Christian Proclamation," in *Sharing Heaven's Music: The Heart of Christian Preaching,* Barry L. Callen, ed. (Nashville: Abingdon Press, 1995), p. 202.

Anything Better Than The Golden Rule?

Luke 6:27-38

A few years ago, I accepted an invitation to preach in a church in upstate New York. The sermon was based on Matthew's version of what we have just heard from the Gospel of Luke: "Turn the other cheek. Give to everyone who begs from you. Pray for those who curse you. And love your enemies." These are nearly impossible words to put into practice, much less hear, and I said as much in my sermon. Jesus is instructing us to take the initiative for making peace, to move beyond revenge and retaliation. We cannot make sense out of these words, I said, unless we see one another from the perspective of God's coming kingdom. The day is coming when there shall be no distinction between "friends" and "enemies." So when the opportunity arises, sometimes we can act as if that day is already here.

That's what I said in my sermon. After the benediction, one person after another shuffled out the door and exchanged greetings. I turned around and went down the hall to hang up my robe, and noticed a young woman waiting for me. She stood with clinched fists and flushed cheeks. "I want you to know," she said, "that I don't agree with a word you said this morning."

"You don't?"

"No, I don't," she said. "The way I see it, you were complicating the teachings of Jesus."

"Was I?"

"Yes, you were," she said. "If we want to follow Jesus, we have to do unto others as we would have them do unto us. That is the essence of what Jesus taught us. As far as I'm concerned, there is nothing better than the Golden Rule. That is all I want to say." With that, she whirled around and stomped away.

She was not the first to sum up the implications of faith with the Golden Rule. About twenty years before the birth of Jesus, the two most prominent Jewish rabbis were named Shammai and Hillel. One day, a Gentile approached the two of them with this challenge: "I challenge you to summarize the teachings of your religion while standing upon one foot."

Shammai dismissed him with the words, "You don't know what you are asking."

The questioner looked at Hillel and gave the challenge again. Hillel stood upon one foot and said, "Whatever is hateful to you, do not do to another. That is the whole law, and all else is commentary."[1]

There is nothing new in Hillel's teaching. The Golden Rule has been around for centuries in one form or another. Jesus did not invent it; he borrowed it from the best ethical traditions of the known world. Confucius taught the Golden Rule in China. Epictetus taught the Golden Rule in ancient Greece. It was a standard teaching of wisdom in many cultures. There is nothing specifically Christian about those words, but there is something genuinely human about them. It has always been a good idea to follow the Golden Rule. Many human problems could be solved if we would "do unto others as we would have them do unto us."

During a recent visit to some family members, I picked up a copy of the local newspaper. It has everything you want in a small town paper: school news, restaurant specials, police reports, and garage sale announcements. On page three, there was a new column; actually it is not a column as much as a transcript. The editors have set up a phone line with an answering machine. They invite their readers to call the answering machine any time day or night and, within a one-minute limit, to say anything that they want to say. The next week, these anonymous comments are published for the whole community to see.

It is stunning to read what people will say anonymously on a telephone. Everybody has a complaint about something or somebody, and that newspaper provides a perfect forum for people to be nasty in public without being held accountable. People can stick it to somebody else because somebody has been sticking it to them. We would have a kinder country if we could simply speak words to others that we would want them to speak to us. If we could treat one another with the same decency that we would want from others, this old tired world would be a much nicer place.

What is so enduring about the Golden Rule is that *it is reciprocal.* The rule keeps us within a relationship to one another. It assumes we live in community. Whatever you want done, you do it for somebody else. However you want to be treated, you treat everybody else that way. If there is a word you want to hear from somebody else, you offer the word first. Living by the Golden Rule means you take other people seriously, particularly in their point of need.

There is a story about a rabbi who was approached by one of his students. The student said, "Rabbi, I love you."

The rabbi said, "Oh, really? Well, do you know what troubles me most?"

The student said, "No, I don't know what troubles you the most."

The rabbi said, "How can you say that you love me if you don't know what troubles me most?"

If I take the Golden Rule seriously, it means that I am going to take you seriously. We share our burdens because we know what it is like to carry a burden. We listen to others because we know how it feels to be ignored. Like the Good Samaritan, we reach out to others because we know what it is like for somebody to pass us by. That's what the Golden Rule is all about. We take others seriously. We put ourselves in others' place. We live as if we have everything in common. Wouldn't it be great if we could live by the Golden Rule?

And yet, I don't know anybody who can live by the Golden Rule. Once in a while, maybe; but not perfectly, and not all the time. If we want proof, we have no further to look than the teachings that lie around the Golden Rule. As some commentators come to this part of Jesus' Sermon on the Plain, they interpret the Golden Rule as a summary of teachings that come immediately before. "Love your enemies," because you want your enemies to love you. "Do good to those who hate you," for you wish their hate to be transformed. "Bless those who curse you. Give to those who beg. Turn the other cheek. Do unto others as you wish they would do unto you."

But there is no automatic connection. If you love your enemies, or act kindly to those who hate you, curse you, and harm you, there is no assurance your enemies will be kind to you. What is missing in the Golden Rule is a means to handle those occasions when the community breaks down, when people cease to take one another seriously, or when people call up the newspaper and leave anonymous complaints without any common responsibility. A good deed for others gives no assurance that others will be good to you. That is the limit of the Golden Rule.

Remember what that woman said to me after that sermon? She said, "There's nothing better than the Golden Rule. That is all we need to do." She could be right: maybe there is nothing better.

But have you ever met somebody who has been able really to live the Golden Rule? I am not talking about being kind to people who are already kind to you, but loving your enemies, truly loving them. I don't mean being nice to other nice people, as if the primary Christian virtue was being nice to nice people; no, I mean acting gracious even when others lash out at you, or acting with kindness to those who are ungrateful and wicked. Is there anybody who can act that way?

Back in the fifth century, there was a British monk named Pelagius. He taught that God would not command us to do something that we are not able to do. "After all," he said, "all of us are basically good people. And if we have a hard time measuring up to God's rules, well, we need to try a little bit harder." It's an appealing idea, which may be why I know a lot of closet Pelagians. Their voices speak up and say:

- "If we could only pull ourselves up by our own bootstraps;
- "If we could only be more productive with our time;
- "If we could only work a little harder;
- "If we could only 'do unto others' a bit more, then we will be good enough for God."

106

There is great appeal to thinking like Pelagius. But it didn't take long for the church to declare such thinking a heresy.

As I said before, there is nothing specifically Christian about the Golden Rule. It is simply a teaching about how we should behave: "Do unto others as you would have them do unto you." The Gospel, on the other hand, is good news about what God has done in the face of our misbehavior. What gathers us here as a church is not an affirmation of human goodness and competence, but rather a celebration of what God has done in the thick of our weakness and incompetence. For what has *God* done? God has loved his enemies. God has been good to those who hate him. God has blessed those who curse him. God has been kind to the ungrateful and the wicked.

We have seen it on the cross where Jesus was hanging. Someone struck Jesus on the cheek, and he offered the other cheek also. Someone took away Jesus' coat, and he did not withhold his shirt. Someone took away all of his goods, and Jesus did not ask for them again. This is what God is like, particularly for those who *do not* do unto others as they wish it done unto them.

Without the cross, the Golden Rule is merely a Silver Suggestion or a Platinum Platitude. Without the revelation of God in the death of Jesus, we are captive to our own advice. It is true that the Golden Rule has been present in many cultures, in many languages, among many peoples. Yet if Jesus came merely to teach people what they already know, then he could have ignored the cross, lived to a ripe old age, never troubled anybody, and sold self-help books. As you know, that's not what happened. "While we were helpless, Christ died for the ungodly ... While we still were sinners Christ died for us" (Romans 5:6-8). Jesus died at the hands of people who thought they didn't need him. He forgave his enemies. He extended the mercy of God to all of us ... in the end that we might become merciful.

A number of years ago, *The New York Times Magazine* told the story of Nicholas Gage and his mother Eleni. Eleni was a Greek peasant who smuggled her son out of the village before he could be "re-educated" by the communist party. As a result, she was tortured and murdered on August 28, 1948.

Thirty-two years later, her son quit his job as a reporter for the *New York Times*. He devoted his time and money to finding his mother's killer. He sifted through government cover-ups and false leads. Eventually he found the person who ordered Eleni's death. His name was Katis.

In a moving account, he tells of going up the path to a seaside cottage, where he sees Katis, fast asleep. He stood and looked at the man who had killed his mother. But as he pondered his revenge, Gage remembered how his mother did not spend the last moments cursing her tormentors; rather, she faced death with courage because she had done her duty to those she loved. "I could have killed Katis," he confessed.

> *"It would have given me relief from the pain that had filled me for so many years. But as much as I want that satisfaction, I have learned that I can't do it. My mother's love, the primary impulse of her life, still binds us together, often surrounding me like a tangible presence. Summoning the hate to kill my enemy would have severed that bridge connecting us. It would have destroyed the part of me that is most like my mother."*[2]

Gage prowled all over Greece, looking to treat somebody else as he felt his mother had been treated. He spent his money trying to give the enemy a taste of his own medicine. Instead he was interrupted by love, a mother's love that made sacrifices for him, a love that was not withheld even in the face of certain death, a love like the love of Christ on the cross.

When we love one another like this, we show ourselves to be children of the Most High God. The promise of the gospel is that God is kind to the ungrateful, the wicked, and the self-sufficient. You have heard it said, "Do to others as you would have them do unto you." But the gospel says, *"Do unto others as God has done unto you."*

Yes, there is something better than the Golden Rule, and it is the marvelous love of God. Love is one trait that marks a church full of God's children. Around here, you might say there is a striking family resemblance.

1. Joseph A. Fitzmyer, *The Gospel According to Luke I-IX* (New York: Doubleday, 1981), p. 639.

2. Quoted by James F. Kay, *Seasons of Grace* (Grand Rapids: Erdmanns, 1994), pp. 71-72. Original source: *New York Times Magazine* 3 April 1983: 20.

Getting It Together

Luke 6:39-49

Hypocrisy. We know it when we see it.

A newspaper recently quoted a congressman. I had to read the article twice to make sure I got it right. In the midst of a debate, an elected official stood to address the House of Representatives. Here's what he said: "Never before have I heard such ill-informed, wimpy, back-stabbing drivel as that just uttered by my respected colleague, the distinguished gentleman from Ohio."

Hypocrisy. We know it when we see it.

Maybe you heard about the leader in another church who was asked to speak to a junior high Sunday school class. The teacher wanted him to talk about the positive aspects of being a Christian, such as how his faith determined his business decisions and set his family priorities. Some of the students began to lose attention.

In an effort to keep their attention, he suddenly stopped, pointed at one boy, and said, "Do you know why people call me a Christian?"

The startled teenager sat up and replied, "Is it because they don't know you?"

Hypocrisy. We know what it looks like. We know what it sounds like. And we cheer when Jesus turns to speak against it. That's what Jesus is doing in the passage we heard this morning.

There are a number of independent teachings in our Scripture text. Each little block of instruction could be treated independently. The thread that stitches them together is hypocrisy, that nearly fatal condition of acting like somebody you're not.

- Why do you see the speck in your neighbor's eye and ignore the log in your own eye?
- You will know them by the fruit they produce. Are figs gathered from thorns or thistles?
- You say, "Lordy, Lordy," but you don't do what I tell you.

At least nineteen times in the gospels, Jesus takes on people whom he calls hypocrites. The Greek word is taken from the acting stage. "Hupocrites" are actors or actresses. They put on a show, supposedly for the benefit of others. They wear costumes and masks, so their appearance does not reflect who they really are. There is a difference between their outward appearance on stage and who they actually are when nobody but God is looking.

According to one wry definition, hypocrites are those "who, professing virtues that they do not respect, secure the advantage of seeming to be what they despise."[1] They appear to be something other than what they actually are.

"Let me take that speck out of your eye." With a self-deprecating air, they mean, "Let me take care of you. Let me point something out to you." All the while they totally ignore their own inability to see clearly. On the surface, it sounds like they want to care; but something else is going on behind the mask.

As one commentator points out, this kind of hypocrisy is all the more unpleasant "because an apparent act of kindness (taking a speck of dirt from somebody's eye) is made the means of inflating our own ego."[2] That is, it looks like these people are trying to help others, when actually they are trying to feel better about themselves. They exalt themselves by pointing out something deficient about their neighbors. Then they try to help others in their weakness from a position of superiority. "Here," they say with transparent deference, "let me help you get that speck out of your eye."

We know it when we see it.

Ever notice? When somebody criticizes you, the criticism usually has to do more with him or her than it has to do with you. Most likely they are flinging their baggage at you rather than carry it themselves.

A woman recently went through some personal difficulties. She said, "When I went through my divorce, the people who gave me the hardest time were people who came from their own troubled households. On the other hand, the people who saved my life were those who knew what it was like to go through something like that, and they helped me come through it alive."

Jesus says: "Take the log out of your eye. Keep your grubby fingers out of the eyes of others, and deal with your own blind spots."

It reminds me of the day when Snoopy was sitting on the roof of his doghouse. Charlie Brown came up and said, "I hear you're writing a book on theology. I hope you have a good title."

Snoopy replied, "I have the perfect title." Then he leaned over his typewriter and typed, "Has It Ever Occurred to You That You Might Be Wrong?"[3]

That's the question for every one of us to ask ourselves if we are ever going to get rid of the lumberyard in our own eyelashes. Jesus uses this ridiculous image to score his point. All of us have no problem turning to another person and seeing faults. All of us have a lot of problems owning up to our own shortcomings and faults. It's difficult to get a proper perspective.

In his commentary on Matthew, Tom Long notes there are two transformations that must occur if we are ever going to be useful to God or anybody else. First, you have to find the wrong in yourself before turning the spotlight on anybody else. You have to face what you spend your whole life avoiding about yourself. Only then, says Long, can you move from self-righteousness to compassion. The good news is that those who deal with their own blindspots can be helpful to others.[4] But it means taking a good, long, honest look at yourself.

A number of years ago, novelist Frederick Buechner dared to tell the story of a day in his own life. He began the book by saying:

> *I am a part-time novelist who happens also to be a part-time Christian because part of the time seems to be the most I can manage to live out my faith: Christian part of the time when certain things seem real and important to me and the rest of the time not Christian in any sense*

that I can believe matters much to Christ or anybody else ... From time to time I find a kind of heroism momentarily possible — a seeing, doing, telling of Christly truth — but most of the time I am indistinguishable from the rest of the herd that jostles and snuffles at the great trough of life. Part-time novelist, Christian, pig.[5]

The honesty is refreshing. Religious people face the endless temptation of thinking they are better than they are. Just when we think we're getting somewhere, when we think we're actually making some spiritual progress, the truth slices like a two-edged sword. And if you don't have a sense of humor about your own foibles, you can drive yourself over the edge. One thing I've noticed about true-blue hypocrites — they are incapable of laughing at themselves.

They ought to know better. Life has a way of unrolling so that all things are revealed. Jesus says, "Look at the results!" Good trees bear good fruit; bad trees have rotten fruit. Build a house on solid ground, and it will survive every storm. Build on a shaky foundation, and sooner or later the whole enterprise will fall apart.

So today we are called upon to get it together: to seek out the truth about ourselves and to trust God to do something positive with what we discover. Jesus has a lot to say to hypocrites, probably because he knows that hypocrites are the only people who can ever pay any attention to him. There isn't a person here who is anything close to what he or she professes.

Through this text, the Risen Lord calls us to move toward a unity of word and deed, a consistency of intention and accomplishment, an integrity between what is seen and what is hidden. It is so easy to mislead ourselves. The evidence of our sin is that we can construct a view of the world that ignores the obstructions of our own making.

When I was a student in seminary, I preached my first sermon to a dozen classmates. It was preaching class, and they were scattered around Miller Chapel. Each of my classmates sat a few pews apart from one another, with clipboards and notebooks on their laps. I did the best I could and put together a sermon on the text

114

where Jesus says, "Don't be anxious! Look at the birds of the air, and the lilies of the field." I stood up with that text and preached my heart out. I wagged my finger and said, "Don't be anxious! Stop fretting! Cease your worry!"

The sermon came to an end. Everybody got out of their pews with their clipboards and gathered in the chancel for a critique. The professor said, "What do we need to say about that sermon?" Nobody said much; I thought, "I really gave it to them today!" I sat there, basking in my own manufactured limelight.

Then somebody said something that I will never forget. In fact, it was so truthful, so on-target, that it forever changed the way that I approach preaching. She said, "Bill, your sermon was full of confidence and power. Even your title is 'Defeating Anxiety.' But as I listened to you today, I found myself wanting to ask, 'Have you ever felt anxious about anything?' "

"Don't get me wrong," she said. "Everything you said in your sermon is true, at least on paper. But it would be easier for me to hear you talk about anxiety, if you could find the courage to tell me about the times when you have known it and gotten through it."

It was more honesty than I expected, but I'm glad for it. She gave me more than her opinion, which would have reduced the feedback to her word against mine, which is always a dead-end street. Rather she pushed me to speak with the kind of integrity that sees life for all of its promises and pitfalls.

God knows we are not the people that we want others to see. There is always a shadow between our intentions and our accomplishments. But God has sent Jesus Christ to save us from our own poor records of achievement. Jesus never had a log in his eye, but he was nailed to a great big piece of timber. And on the cross, he has taken away every sin. In his mercy, every speck and blemish has already been removed. Thanks to Jesus, we have been freed to serve God without needing to feel inadequate. All we have to do is trust that it's true.

And along the way, we learn how to love and laugh. A woman named Lois volunteered to help with a congregational mailing. As she scanned the address list, she noted a lot of people had drifted away from the life of the church. She picked up the phone and began to call them. "We've been missing you in all kinds of ways. Why don't you come back next Sunday?"

She called one man, and got nowhere. The next week, she called him again with the same result. The following week she tried again. Finally he said, "Don't you get it? I'm not going back to that church. There are too many hypocrites in the congregation."

Lois laughed, and she said, "Yeah, you're right. We have a church full of hypocrites. And we always have room for one more."

The man began to laugh. The next week, he was sitting in the fourth pew. After that, he was back almost every Sunday. Most of the time he had a smile on his face.

That is a picture of the gospel working itself out through us. None of us measures up to the righteousness of God, but all of us are held up by the mercy of God. Each one of us must work through that mercy, admitting the moments when we could not see, when we did not act, when we turned out to be something less than we were created to be. This morning Jesus is saying, in effect, "Before you point any fingers at anybody else, first take a long look in the mirror. Stand there and keep looking, until you know that you stand only by the grace and good humor of God."

Today he tells us to give up our incessant criticism of others. He challenges us to stop reading other peoples' situations through our own lenses, and start paying attention to the places where our own lives have gone out of focus. He teaches us to stand on something more secure than the shifting sands of self-affirmation. We can stand firm, instead, on Christ the Rock, who has enough mercy and forgiveness for all of us hypocrites.

And blessed are you when you laugh at yourself. For your laughter is God's opportunity.

---

1. Ambrose Bierce, *The Devil's Dictionary* (New York: Dover Publications, 1993), p. 53. Slightly altered, so that men and women can be included in the definition.

2. John R. W. Stott, *Christian Counter-Culture: The Message of the Sermon on the Mount* (Downers Grove, Ill.: InterVarsity Press, 1978), p. 178.

3. Charles M. Schulz, *And the Beagles and the Bunnies Shall Lie Down Together: The Theology in Peanuts* (New York: Holt, Rinehart and Winston, 1984).

4. Thomas G. Long, *Matthew* (Louisville: Westminster John Knox, 1997), pp. 77-78.

5. Frederick Buechner, *The Alphabet of Grace* (New York: Harper & Row, Publishers, Inc., 1970), pp. vii-viii.

Beyond Our Sight, Within Our Hearing

Luke 9:28-36 (37-43)

I wonder what they were thinking as they started up the mountain.

Peter, James, and John were tagging along. I'm sure Jesus was a few steps ahead. After all, he was the only one who knew where they were going. Those three disciples had put in a lot of miles. Every one of those miles was spent following wherever he went.

It had been that way since the first day, when they got in step behind him on level ground. Jesus was walking around the lakeshore, snatching them one at a time. From that day forward, they spent some time down below on the level ground. They heard Jesus teach, and they were just as astounded as everybody else was. They saw Jesus heal, lifting up the lame and cleaning up the lepers. As saviors go, he was busy all the time, down on the plains and in the valleys. Now he decided to climb up the mountain, first turning to the three to say, "Come, follow me."

We don't know what they were thinking. Did they know he had once climbed a mountain before?

Right after his baptism, he headed for the hills. One day he was so high up, he had a good view of all the kingdoms of the world. The buildings glistened with glory. Jesus could sense the authority and power of the world. Just then, trouble struck. Jesus had to fend off a liar who told him, "This could all be yours. Just sign on the dotted line."

"Get out of here," Jesus said.

Jesus had been on the mountain before. We don't know if the disciples knew anything about that.

What's more, we don't know if the three of them knew that the mountain was his favorite place to pray. As was his custom, Jesus climbed up high to speak to God. Once he went up a mountain and spent a whole night in prayer (Luke 6:12). Nobody told him to do it. It was something he wanted to do. While he was there, he named the twelve people whom he needed in his inner circle. Three of them, of course, were Peter, James, and John.

The irony is not lost on us: those three disciples follow Jesus up the mountain. They slant up one side, then turn on the switchback. In that journey, as they go higher and higher, they approach the kind of place where Jesus had first chosen them in prayer.

But what was going through their heads? We cannot say for sure. One thing's for certain: They had no clue what was coming. Jesus was always a few steps ahead of them.

As Luke tells the story, he says Jesus began to pray. Just then, something began to happen of Old Testament proportions. His face began to shine — just like Moses on another mountain. His clothes were cleansed whiter than snow. And a cloud rolled in, overshadowing the whole group. Suddenly the walls of time and space broke down, and the two greatest characters of the Jewish Scriptures appeared. They began to chat with Jesus as if he was their contemporary.

What did they see? Luke can't quite say. The words aren't adequate. "The appearance of his face changed. His clothes became dazzling white." That's all he can describe. The Jesus whom they had grown accustomed to seeing was changed somehow, becoming in appearance like a shaft of light.

Something like that may not happen when you pray, but it happened to Jesus. Most of us don't have the words to make much sense of it.

Madeleine L'Engle, the great Christian writer, says that's one of the reasons why we tend to avoid this story. In her words:

> *The Christian holiday which is easiest for us is Christmas, because it touches on what is familiar; and the story of the young man and woman who were turned away from the inn, and had a baby in a stable, surrounded by*

gentle animals, is one we have known always. I doubt
if many two- or three-year-olds are told at their mother's
knee about the Transfiguration ... And so, because the
story of Christmas is part of our folklore, we pay more
attention to its recognizableness than to the fact that
the tiny baby in the manger contained the power which
created galaxies and set the stars in their courses.

She concludes by saying:

We are not taught much about the wilder aspects of
Christianity. But these are what artists have wrestled
with throughout the years.[1]

Perhaps an artist ought to set this story in stained glass. It is that kind of story: glossy, unreasonable, and slightly out of focus. Even then, there's no promise that we can capture the moment.

Peter tried as best he could. He said, "Lord, it is good for us to be here. Just say the word, I will pitch three tents up here — one for Moses, one for Elijah, and one for you." But no sooner were the words out of his mouth, still hanging in the air like a cartoon balloon, when a Voice within the cloud cut him off and began to speak. As far as we know, Peter never got a chance to pitch those tents.

That's not to say, however, that the church has not filled the void throughout the centuries. The traditional site for the Transfiguration is Mount Tabor, a high mountain in the north country of Israel. Over the years, the church has gone where Peter could not go, and we have built what he could not build.

- Helena, mother of Constantine, built a sanctuary in the top of Mount Tabor in 326 A.D.
- By the end of the sixth century, three churches stood on the mountaintop, one each for Jesus, Moses, and Elijah.
- More shrines were built there over the next 400 years, and Saladin destroyed all in 1187.
- A fortress built in 1212 was destroyed by the end of the thirteenth century. The summit was abandoned for another

six hundred years, until a Greek Orthodox community built a monastery.

- Some time later, the Franciscans built a Latin basilica on the highest point of the summit, where they now maintain worship services and a website.[2]

The problem, of course, is that we have never been able to capture the event of the transfiguration. We can build shrine after shrine, but that merely reduces the truth of the transfiguration to a distant memory. No, a story like this is too enormous, too truthful, and too unmanageable. All a preacher like me can do is to tell the story, and point in the same direction where it is pointing.

Jesus climbs a high mountain with Peter, James, and John. When they get to the top, something happened to him, and they saw it. He remains the same Lord whom they know and love; yet they realize how radically different he is from them. The same Jesus who became like us in every way is revealed as someone far beyond our comprehension. There's nothing about this moment that you could ever call "helpful." Instead it points us to the transcendent mystery of God, a mystery which is always beyond our grip.

I was listening to a radio show on a Christian station. It was springtime, and a happy announcer was trying very hard to apply this story to our lives. He said something like, "We need to pay attention to those moments when we see things in a new way. Like when we observe the butterfly we never saw before. Or the child's smile. Or when we have a new thought that changes our perception."

I turned the dial and murmured, "Oh, be quiet. Don't tell me about me or you or the butterflies. Speak to me of God. Tell me something that makes my jaw drop. Bend my knees in worship; and should I refuse, break my knees with holy splendor."

Whatever happened to *awe*? This is worship, after all, and before worship is ever helpful to us, worship should direct our attention to the God who is worthy of our worship. I don't know about you, but I want to hear about a God so holy that my eyebrows get singed during the sermon. I want to know about a Jesus for whom it is no big deal to bust down the divisions of time and space, so that he can talk with Moses and Elijah whenever he wishes. I hunger for a kind of worship that knocks me off my feet, precisely because it points to the Presence which we cannot manage, control, or even count on with any predictability. Is that too much to ask? Another preacher said it best when he asked:

> *What if the church serves people, not as a market transaction, but because it is the people of God? What if our choir works hard on their anthem, not because they hope you will like it and be inspired by it but because the choir knows that we are called to be a sign, a signal, a foretaste, a beachhead of God's Kingdom in the world? What if I'm preaching this sermon, not because I think it's uppermost on your list of weekly wants, but rather because I believe this is what God wants? What you get out of what is done here should not be as great a concern among us as fidelity to the peculiar nature of God's Kingdom.*
>
> *What is the greatest service the church can render the world? Perhaps the service we render is not necessarily what the world thinks it needs. But the church is not only about meeting my needs but also about rearranging my needs, giving me needs I would never have known had I not come to church.*[3]

With no help from his disciples or us, Jesus was transfigured. We caught a glimpse of his glory, but we could not capture it. We heard an awesome voice but we could not institutionalize it. All we could do is bend our knees, point in awe, and listen for the Voice to speak. The word that best describes all this is *worship*.

There was a congregation somewhere in the Midwest who suffered a severe blizzard one winter. The snow was high. Even the mail did not get through for a week. That meant the pastor and congregation had no clue what was the denominational emphasis for that week. They were accustomed to being told by the central office of the denomination that it was United Nations Sunday, or the Festival of the Christian Home Sunday, or some other thematic day.

According to the tale, an embarrassed pastor stood before the congregation that Sunday and apologized for the lack of information. Then he announced, "In the absence of any other reason for gathering, we will just worship the Lord."[4]

---

1. Madeleine L'Engle, *Walking on Water: Reflections on Faith and Art* (Wheaton, IL: Harold Shaw Publishers, 1980) 80-1.

2. The site can be reached at http://www.christusrex.org/www1/ofm/san/tab00mn/html

3. "On Not Meeting People's Needs in Church," William Willimon, Duke University Chapel, 6 July 1997.

4. Attributed to Halford Luccock.

Books In This Cycle C Series

GOSPEL SET
Praying For A Whole New World
Sermons For Advent/Christmas/Epiphany
William G. Carter

Living Vertically
Sermons For Lent/Easter
John N. Brittain

Changing A Paradigm — Or Two
Sermons For Sundays After Pentecost (First Third)
Glenn E. Ludwig

Topsy-Turvy: Living In The Biblical World
Sermons For Sundays After Pentecost (Middle Third)
Thomas A. Renquist

Ten Hits, One Run, Nine Errors
Sermons For Sundays After Pentecost (Last Third)
John E. Berger

FIRST LESSON SET
The Presence In The Promise
Sermons For Advent/Christmas/Epiphany
Harry N. Huxhold

Deformed, Disfigured, And Despised
Sermons For Lent/Easter
Carlyle Fielding Stewart III

Two Kings And Three Prophets For Less Than A Quarter
Sermons For Sundays After Pentecost (First Third)
Robert Leslie Holmes

What If What They Say Is True?
Sermons For Sundays After Pentecost (Middle Third)
John W. Wurster

A Word That Sets Free
Sermons For Sundays After Pentecost (Last Third)
Mark Ellingsen

SECOND LESSON SET
You Have Mail From God!
Sermons For Advent/Christmas/Epiphany
Harold C. Warlick, Jr.

Hope For The Weary Heart
Sermons For Lent/Easter
Henry F. Woodruff

A Hope That Does Not Disappoint
Sermons For Sundays After Pentecost (First Third)
Billy D. Strayhorn

Big Lessons From Little-Known Letters
Sermons For Sundays After Pentecost (Middle Third)
Kirk W. Webster

Don't Forget This!
Robert R. Kopp
Sermons For Sundays After Pentecost (Last Third)